EXPAT PARTNER

EXPAT
Staying Active
PARTNER
& Finding Work

Carine Bormans
Marie Geukens

LANNOO CAMPUS

This book was originally published as *Partner van een expat? Zo blijf je actief, zo vind je werk*, LannooCampus, 2020.

D/2020/45/133 – ISBN 978 94 014 6795 7 – NUR 800

Cover design: Studio Lannoo
Interior design: Wendy De Haes
Translation: Ingrid Van Waes, Graham Muir
Photograph page 105: Saskia Vanderstichele

LannooCampus Publishers is a subsidiary of Lannoo Publishers,
the book and multimedia division of Lannoo Publishers nv.

LannooCampus Publishers
Vaartkom 41 box 01.02
3000 Leuven
Belgium
www.lannoocampus.com

P.O. Box 23202
1100 DS Amsterdam
Netherlands

Contents

Preface

Life consists of many mornings

Malian saying

What would it be like to live and work in another country? Away from the daily drudgery of home, the cold weather, the annoying boss, the hectic pace. A new life in another country. Maybe not forever, but for a while? Absolutely! Many people dream about it. Perhaps you and your partner have already taken the first step and are looking for a job in development cooperation, in a multinational corporation, or in the service of your Ministry of Foreign Affairs. And then one day your partner says: 'Pack your bags: we're about to leave.' You feel euphoric yet apprehensive. Perhaps the dream is on hold now that you have a good job yourself. Maybe your initially enthusiastic reply — 'I'm so happy for you!' — quickly becomes a doubtful 'But what am I going to do?'

We have written this book for you, the expat partner. Research and personal stories underline the importance of embarking on a foreign adventure as a happy partner. In these times of gender equality, a career – and almost everyone has a job nowadays – undoubtedly contributes to that happiness. NetExpat's *Relocating Partner Survey Report 2018* makes this crystal clear. Furthermore, according to HR managers the main reason why individuals turn down an international assignment is because the partner does not want to give up his/her career. This is especially the case for male expat partners (around 10% of expat partners are male). In the same report the top response (71%) to the question 'What are the most common reasons for failed foreign assignments?' is 'an unhappy, non-integrated partner'. It is therefore crucial that you, the expat partner, are also comfortable with the overseas posting.

These days, most couples take decisions about a life abroad jointly. Often, the partner is just as highly skilled as the expat: according to the same NetExpat survey, 82% of partners have a bachelor's, master's or doctoral degree. For the recent batch of expats the figure rises to almost 91%. Expats and partners increasingly treat each other as equals, but if one of them decides to accept a job abroad, the other might feel that their role is of secondary importance. You will have plenty of things to keep you busy: adapting to a new culture, moving to a new house, a new school — and curriculum — for the children, the home and its interior decoration, work permits, the recognition of diplomas. This can lead to pressure for the individual and the couple. These are all aspects of the relocation in which the added value of the partner cannot and should not be underestimated. To help you with the challenges of a life as an expat, you will find a list of suggested reading at the end of the book.

This no-nonsense book is about jobs, jobs, jobs. For many, this seems key to feel satisfied and integrated. Clearly the expat partner will have many questions when the possibility of a move abroad becomes real. What if you stop working here? Will you find work there? If so, what kind of work? What impact will the move have on your professional development? You might know what you want, but not how to achieve it. You know you want to work, but how do you decide whether or not to accept a particular job? How can you be more conscious about the choices? Based on a pie chart containing five pieces, this book is a step-by-step guide to choosing the specific job that fits you at a particular stage in your life. Each slice of pie represents one specific aspect of what a job entails: depending on where you are in life, you will find some aspects more important than others. This book is designed to help you to think clearly about how and why to look for work when you move abroad as an expat partner.

The book is also intended as a tool for coaches, trainers and supervisors of expats and their partner. It can help HR departments when sending staff abroad, be it in the public or private sectors. Supporting expats and their partner takes many forms. One employee or partner might benefit from group sessions, while another may need individual coaching. This self-help book provides advice in either case.

The pie model is a concept of Carine Bormans. As an expat partner, she has been travelling the world with her husband, who is a diplomat, for more than thirty years. As a Family Officer in the Belgian Ministry of Foreign Affairs, she has informed and guided many expat families based on this simple model, which can help expat partners in their search for a balance between moving abroad and pursuing a career.

Marie Geukens was first exposed to the model at one of Carine's workshops, and immediately saw its potential. Before long, they put their heads together. With her background as an editor and expat partner, Marie proved to be the ideal teammate to turn Carine's ideas into a book. Throughout their careers, they have met many expat partners. Some of them – consciously or unconsciously – have implemented this model. This book also describes the experiences of expat partners. For privacy reasons, names and locations have been changed.

What is it you want?

Many can benefit from this model: those who make a career choice, become unemployed, retire, or emigrate. The model allows you to look at work from different angles: the meaning of work is interpreted in different ways. This model is all about the value you attribute to your work.

Expat partners are the central theme in this book. Dictionaries generally describe an expatriate as someone who has citizenship in at least one country, but who is living and working for a certain period of time in another. That person could choose to reside in another country out of conviction, or for the sake of adventure. It can involve different periods in different countries. An expat usually sets out with the idea that one day, he or she will return home.

In the twenty-first century, there is much pressure to have financial independence. Many expat partners are therefore happy to have some sort of career whilst abroad. The French expat organisation Expat Communication carried out an extensive survey of expat partners.

Alix Carnot, their head of Expat Intelligence and International Careers, analysed the results in her book *Chéri(e) on s'expatri(e)!*. To the question: 'Is it inevitable that one of the two will give up their career while abroad?', 40% of the couples interviewed replied that they both managed to have jobs. It is a long and winding road, but it is possible. Other significant statistics in the book confirm stereotypical gender inequalities: among expat partners over 50, only 10% are men. This is not age-related, because among 30-year-olds, this is 11%. 91% of expat partners are women, 60% of whom do not work during an overseas posting. It remains mainly a female issue, but it is not our intention to exclude men from this book.

Priorities: do you have any?

You can apply the pie model when you are faced with a decision. The exercise requires you to set priorities. Your options thus become clearer and you can make more informed choices. These not only depend on the stage you have reached in your life, and your environment, but also on what is important in your life *at that time*. Stages of life change us. So does spending part of your life in a different culture. 20% of expat partners decide not to work: instead, they consciously choose to focus on the children, or to make more time for themselves, or to get to know their host country more thoroughly. The remaining 80% look for work. The main reasons are to avoid gaps in the CV and to keep competencies up to date.

The impact of work on your life

According to the Collins Cobuild English dictionary, 'to work' means, among other things:

> *work (works, working, worked)*
> *1. Spending time and effort doing a task that needs to be done, or trying to achieve something;*
> *2. To have a job, usually paid; to do the things you are paid or required to do in your job.*

This book focuses on the second definition: you perform labour and are remunerated for it. Work brings with it a range of benefits: salary, health insurance, pension, a collegiate workplace, and status, ... For people from developed countries, this is the norm. You enjoy the certainty and it makes your life structured and safe.

The moment you stop working, for example because you are going abroad, those benefits stop. That can be scary or disruptive. How do you cope? Can you replicate that structure? If so, how?

How to use this book

The book comprises three main parts. In the first, we explain the five aspects of work – the five slices of pie. Each aspect involves specific questions, to which you need to find the answers, either on your own or with your partner. Some of you may want to consult an expert. To make it more concrete, we have included personal testimonials from a selection of expat partners. This is one step closer to a new reality.

In the second part, we use our own personal stories to illustrate how we have applied the model in our own expat life — sometimes whether we wanted to or not. Work is essential for both of us, but because our personalities differ, we attach different importance to the aspects of work. This provides a broad picture of obstacles and opportunities, frustration and courage, luck, and conscious choices.

And finally, Part 3 deals with 'flow'. This was essential because work gives us both great satisfaction. You experience flow during an activity when you forget about time – and yourself – and at the same time thoroughly enjoy yourself. You use all your skills when you carry out this activity and you know that you will successfully complete the task. These are 'optimal experiences', enabling you to lead a full and rewarding life. Work offers many such moments. What if these disappear because you have to give up your job? Here, too, we want to contextualise things so that you can experience your flow again.

The book is also a plea to view an opportunity overseas with an open mind and level-headed realism. After all, life is about more than just work. Working in a new environment, in another country or situation, can be enriching and fulfilling. This book is intended not only for those who are unsure about the prospect of travelling as an expat partner, but also for those who are already abroad. It may be that, after reading this and reviewing your priorities clearly, you decide not to go abroad. That of course is a legitimate choice. But above all, we hope to prepare you for a successful expat experience. Either way, we do not regret our own – at times adventurous – expat life.

PART 1

What does work mean

The five aspects

The five aspects of an active professional career have an impact on your life. Depending on the stage of life you have reached, one aspect will be more important than another. To make the choice that suits you best, it is crucial that you have a full understanding of all five aspects, and what they mean to you.

Salary

If you work as an employee, you receive a salary. At the very least, this will be the minimum salary, but for most expat partners it is a lot higher before they go abroad. The survey by Expat Communications published in *Le livre blanc* shows that 72% of expat partners have a master's degree. In her book *Conjoint d'expatrié: votre carrière continue!* expat expert Stéphanie Talleux states that 54% of expat partners working abroad are overqualified and their potential often remains under-utilised. If you stop work to go abroad, you will become financially dependent on the expat, unless you have other sources of income.

Social and financial securities

If you work, especially as an employee, you are entitled to social security with specific rights such as the accrual of a pension, invalidity benefits, unemployment insurance, health insurance, etc. These rights were acquired during the twentieth century and codified in labour and pension legislation. They differ from country to country. They offer financial and social support and are vital to one's peace of mind. If you stop accruing these benefits, there will be long-term consequences.

Developing professional skills

When you work you develop professional skills. This process continues throughout your career. If you stop working, you stop learning and developing specific skills related to your job — not only the necessary knowledge and technological competence, but also team spirit and collaboration, negotiating, analysing work-related issues and finding solutions.

Social contacts and the need for structure

Parents, school, after-school activities provide a strict time-scedule from our birth onwards. During our student days, this structure is often much looser — which is not always an advantage. But in the labour market we need to conform to working hours, at least for most jobs. If you lose your job, you lose some structure in your life and find yourself with a lot of spare time on your hands. Many people cannot handle this: a self-imposed structure and filling the day or week is not easy.

Along with a fixed work structure, do not underestimate the importance of daily contact with work colleagues. Chatting over a morning coffee, dropping in on a colleague, working in a team: these social contacts are an essential part of our life. If you stop working, the daily and weekly routine, as well as social interaction, will disappear.

Identity

Identity is perhaps the most challenging aspect. It involves so much. If you ask people, 'What do you do?', the most common reply is 'I am a [insert the name of their profession here]'. Society expects that answer. People with a specific profession, such as doctors, journalists, dentists, nurses, diplomats or managers, often identify first and foremost with their job. This is not the case for everyone. But if you strongly identify yourself with your profession, discontinuing your professional activity will be even more challenging.

All in good time

Every decision revolves around that one key question: what motivates you in a job? Why do you want that job? Or, to put it another way, which aspect attracts you the most?

If you are planning on a foreign adventure with your expat and you want to preserve all five aspects, your initial situation is more complicated and your choices are more limited. Depending on the profession, it should be possible for some individuals to fulfil all five aspects whilst abroad. But for the majority this will not be the case.

Yet working abroad is easier than you might imagine. It depends on what you want to get out of the job. After all, with a clear understanding of what each aspect means to you at that point in your life, you can opt for a specific job opportunity more consciously and more clearly.

The most important question here is: 'What motivates you to work?'.

According to Alix Carnot, continuity in the CV and retention of skills are the key motivators that drive expat partners to finding work. Of these, 33% do so because they want a degree of independence, 11% because they want to maintain their standard of living, and 8% because they feel the need to be part of a collective endeavour. She continues: 'These figures are about expat partners who do not need two incomes to survive while abroad. Their motivation is mainly due to concern about finding a job again on their return home and the need for their own project. That being so, is a local job the best way to safeguard your employability and self-development? In the constantly changing context of the culture shock at the start of the posting overseas, motivation is often vague and variable.' We believe you can mitigate this by considering beforehand which aspect(s) of work you find important at the time. You can do this by using Carine's pie model.

Which slice of the pie remains on your plate?

Each aspect is of equal importance. That is why we place them in juxtaposed triangles or wedges. This is how a pie is created. Now the insight begins. Ask yourself the question 'Which piece of the pie do I want?', and make your choice.

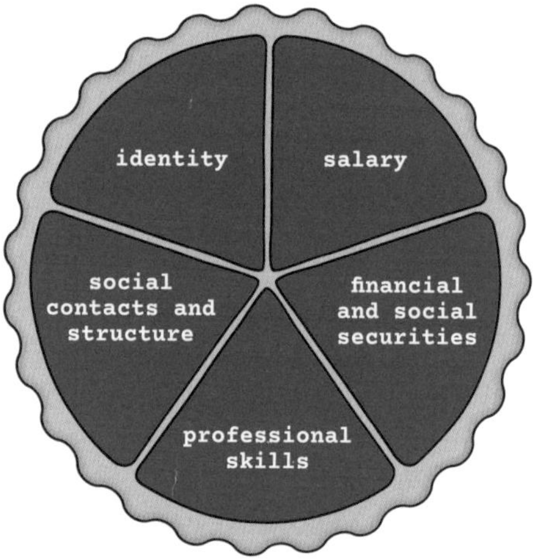

The pie and its five aspects

The wedges that remain on the dish are important: you will want to keep them. Those of lower (or no) importance can be put in the refrigerator. This requires you to set your priorities.

An example:

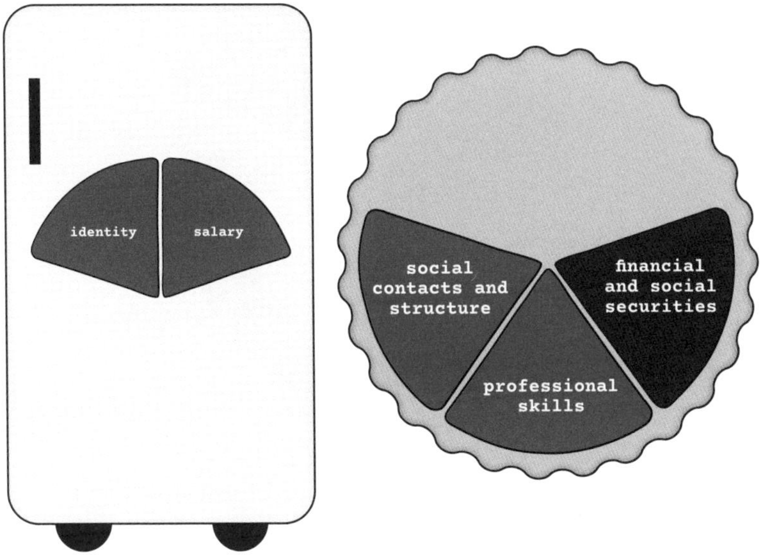

The aspect that you have already acquired and remains important is coloured in black. The aspect that you are striving for is in red. In this way you can identify your objectives.

Salary

Money. Do you want it?
'Yes', says Marie. 'No', says Carine.

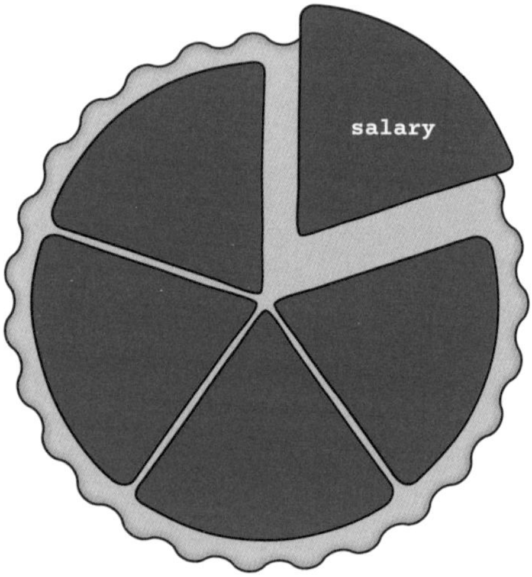

Clearly you want to be paid for your work. The primary function of money is to pay your bills, but it also represents appreciation and recognition. The purpose of a salary is thus two-fold: as a source of income and savings on the one hand; and as social recognition for the achievements provided on the other. Let us take a closer look.

Spending and saving

You work and thus receive a salary or some other form of compensation. In our society men and women have an equal right to work. This can be as an employee, employer or self-employed person. It is also possible from home. Performance is rewarded by payment. You use that money to pay your bills, to make your life more agreeable, to save. If you move abroad, your work and your income can often be lost – unless you have other sources of income, such as rent. According to Alix Carnot the greatest challenge for 61% of expat partners is the loss of financial independence. You become financially dependent on the person for whom you give up your job, and that can cause friction.

How do you deal with this as a couple? Several issues need to be addressed. Do you each have your own bank account, or does everything go into a joint account? Will that remain the case, or not? Do you split everything fifty-fifty or is there a different apportionment? Do you ask your partner to help cover your expenses? If so, on a weekly or monthly basis? How do you handle savings? And what about when you return? What if you, as the partner, can no longer work, or have to take on a less well-paid job as a result of your career break?

There are many questions to consider and discuss, because downsizing to one income has an effect on the entire family. According to a 2018 NetExpat survey, most expat partners find their salary significant (56%) or critical (13%) for the family's income. 31% indicate that their salary is irrelevant. We should, however, make a distinction between short- and long-term assignments abroad. The second family income plays a more crucial role when it comes to a short appointment of, say, a few months. Longer assignments often involve more attractive financial rewards for the expat, to the extent that this can reduce the importance of the second income. According to the survey, if the move abroad is permanent the second income becomes a necessity. In addition, we noticed that the younger the employee, the more important the second income: not only is the expat's salary not as high, but there are also no reserves built up from a double income.

Salary as social recognition for the services provided

The reality is that a surgeon earns more than a bus driver. Advanced studies, specific professions and greater responsibilities usually attract a corresponding income. Generally, you will not want to work if you do not get paid for it, or if the payment is insufficient. There is a general acknowledgement that, if you have fulfilled a certain work-related task, you are entitled to be paid for it. This is an important recognition. Only exceptionally are we willing to work for free. Salary also gives you status, within your own family, with your friends, and in the wider world in which you move.

Working for a lower wage is often regarded as an injustice and a loss of status. Research by Yvonne McNulty, Professor of Social Sciences at the University of Singapore, shows that unpaid or underpaid work is unattractive to many expat partners. Some resented that they were 'supporting the local citizens for free', and perceived that they themselves were 'not good enough to be employed, pay my taxes and be given my independence'. Most expat partners look for work abroad to develop themselves or to retain or improve professional skills. These two objectives do not necessarily require a salary for them to be achieved. It is important to agree with your partner how to mitigate the loss of one income.

For example, you can meet these objectives through voluntary work. And even though this is not a plea for voluntary work it might, in your specific situation, be an option to do temporary unpaid work, or to work for a lower salary. Try to not lose sight of the bigger picture and not exclude this possibility.

The change in financial situation is one of the factors that causes stress in a relationship. According to McNulty's research, the expat's long working hours and the resulting loneliness and isolation of the expat partner are the top causes of stress. Giving up one's career, the changing dynamics within the relationship and the loss of one's social network can also cause tension. Many experienced expat partners consider a 'strong relationship' to be central to dealing with the challenges of life abroad. A healthy relationship is based on strong mutual understanding. Money plays a crucial part. The bottom line is that you keep communication open and discuss these delicate issues with your partner.

> If you want to work abroad and earn the same salary in order to cover your expenses and savings as well as receive the same recognition as in your home country, your choices are more limited. By considering options such as working for a lower salary or as a volunteer, you broaden your options. Change the logic behind your career planning and look at all the possibilities that present themselves.
>
> Take the bull by the horns and discuss the matter. You need to talk to your partner about how you feel about the changing financial situation and how you can learn to deal with it.

Ask yourself a few questions:

- How important is a salary to you?
- How much value do you attach to the size of the salary? How important is it to your partner?
- What is the effect on family income if you set aside the 'salary' aspect? Can you still provide for your family and maintain the desired quality of life?
- How do the new financial agreements influence your relationship? What changes?
- What would your partner think if you were to take a job with a lower wage? Or one with no pay?
- How do you regard someone who works for free? Is that also 'work'? What level of recognition do you give to this work?

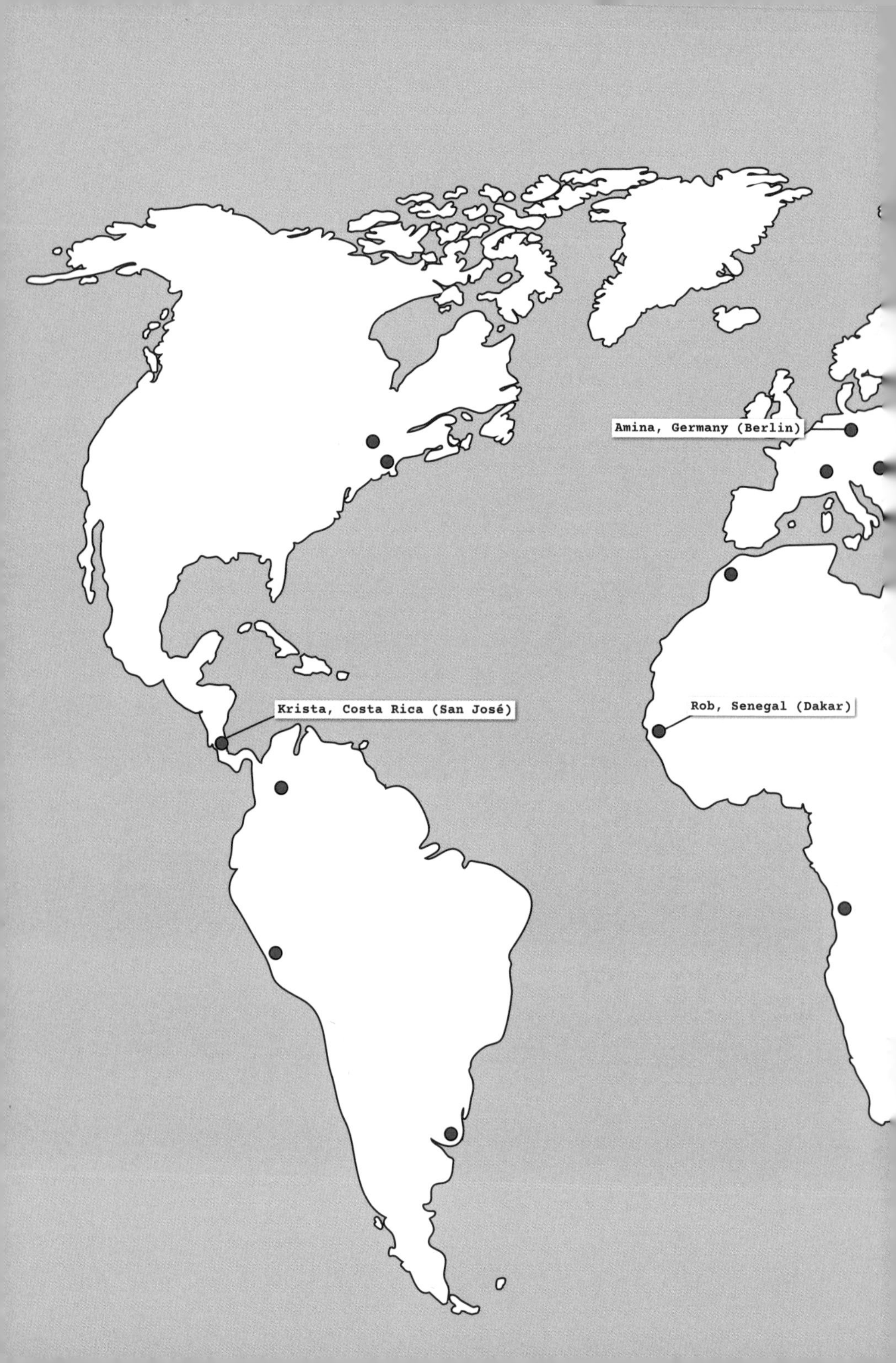
Amina, Germany (Berlin)
Krista, Costa Rica (San José)
Rob, Senegal (Dakar)

– Stories from the field –

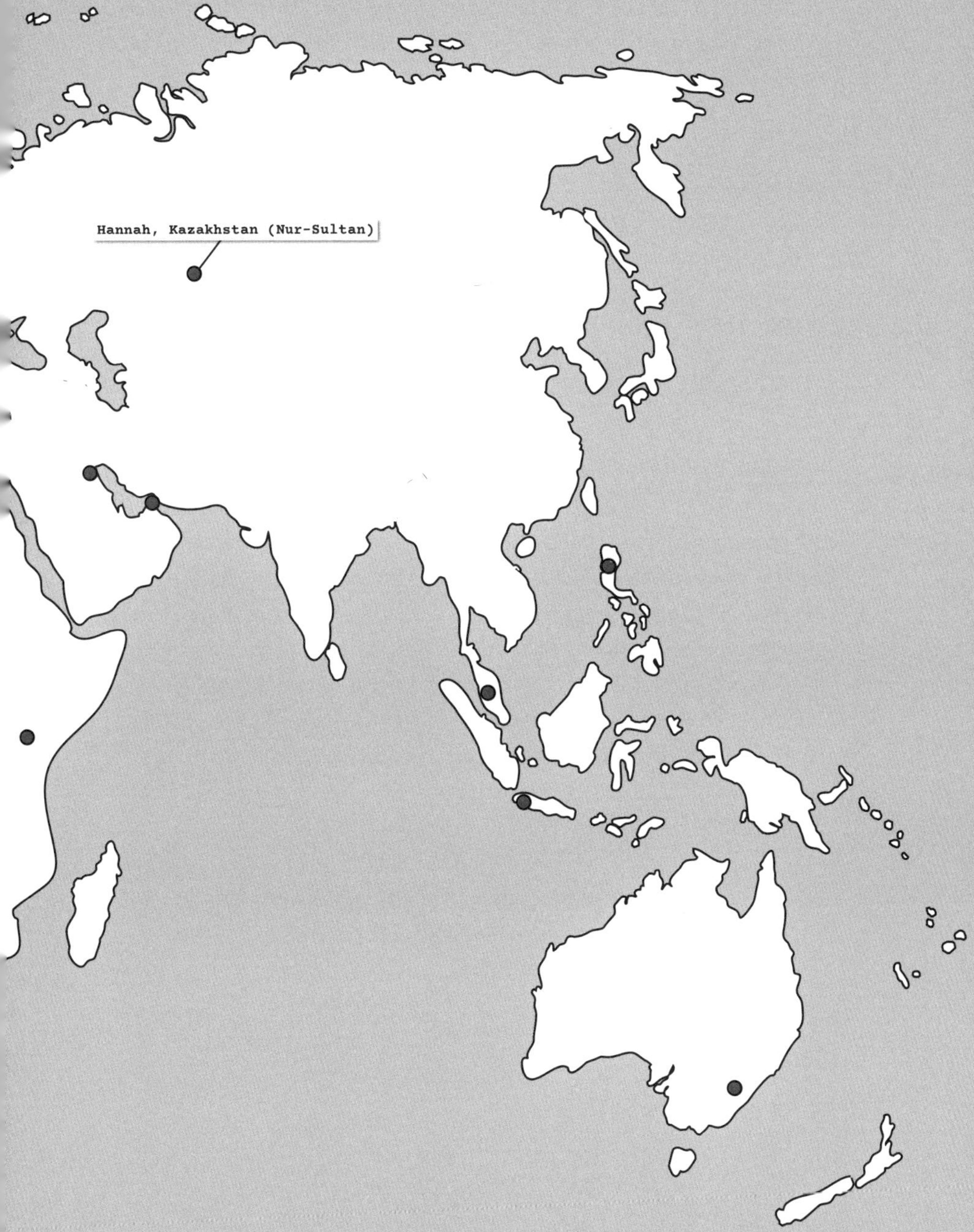

Hannah in Nur-Sultan, Kazakhstan

During one of Carine's workshops, expat partners discuss their experience of working abroad. There is outrage when the following question is asked: 'Who wants to work for 300 euros a month?' 'Certainly not!' 'No, never!' But Hannah says, 'Actually, that's what I earn right now.' As a designer, she continues to design handbags, scarves and other accessories during her stay in Nur-Sultan, and sells them through her webshop. When she deducts her costs, her net income is on average 300 euros per month.

For Hannah, being able to continue to develop her professional skills is essential. It is a higher priority than salary.

Krista in San José, Costa Rica

Krista and Marc have a lovely family with three children. Marc works as a financial adviser for a multinational, Maria manages the household and the children do well at school. Everything runs smoothly. But Krista becomes bored and dissatisfied. She finds it hard not having her own salary, even though Marc shares everything with her. Krista is looking for a paid job. She has a master's degree in urbanisation, but soon realises that it is far from easy to find work in that area. So, any job will do. Through the newsletter of the French expat community, Krista learns that there is a vacancy at the administration department of the French school. She jumps at the chance.

Krista's enthusiasm convinces management that she is the right person for the job. While acknowledging that the job is below her skill level, a salary is her top priority.

Rob in Dakar, Senegal

Rob works for the Dutch Ministry of Foreign Affairs and is passionate about his job. He meets a French diplomat, they connect and become a couple. Rob has a temporary contract and she has a permanent job. When his partner is assigned a job in Dakar, Rob follows her. As an expat partner he starts looking for a job. But this is difficult. He finds work as a trainee at the Dutch embassy in the hope of expanding his network and to find a job that comes with a salary.

Rob chooses to develop his professional skills and social life, hoping to find a paid job.

A year later, there is a vacancy in the embassy's administrative department. It does not fully match Rob's profile. He has a choice to make: a paid job below his level, or voluntary work while looking for a different paid job? The latter looks risky. So Rob opts for the paid position. Thanks to his efforts, Rob acquires some diplomatic tasks in addition to the more mundane administrative duties.

At that point in time, Rob puts a salary first. A paid job offers him the social recognition he needs. He wants 'real work'.

Amina in Berlin, Germany

Amina has lived abroad for eleven years and is happy that she had the time to raise the children. As a trained vet she found it difficult to get a job. Now she is back in Germany, her home country. The children have either left home or are on the verge of doing so. One works, the other two are students. She has a lot of time on her hands. She is 46 and feels as if it is 'now or never'. If she is to return to the labour market, there is no time to waste. She lacks experience as a vet. But she can organise better than anyone and has learnt several languages whilst overseas. Soon she finds work through a temp office as a guide for tour groups visiting Berlin. Sometimes she works at a trade fair or conference. The work is varied. Amina decides not to become self-employed because too much paperwork is involved. Part of her wages goes to the interim office.

By working through a temp office, Amina earns less, but she has work. That is her priority: not the size of the salary, but the fact that she has one.

Hannah, Rob, Krista and Amina have different motives, but all four want to earn money. The amount does not really matter. That choice is determined by the context on the one hand and by their own priorities on the other. Every decision is personal. It is important to know your own priorities at a specific stage in your life.

Financial and social securities

'I can't live on quicksand.' CARINE

'As long as my marriage feels solid, it seems unimportant to me.' MARIE

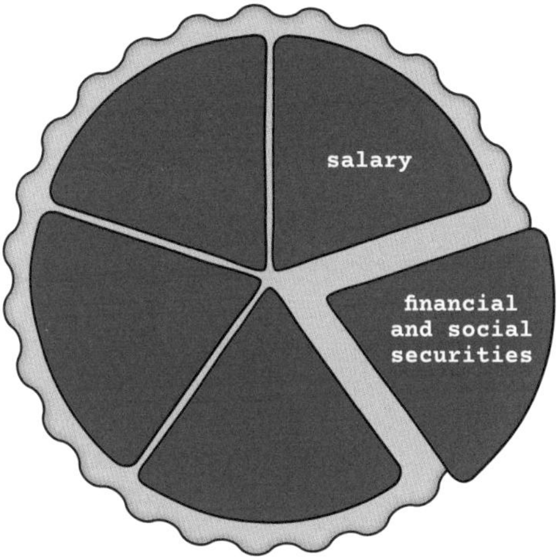

A country protects its workers through legislation. Labour laws determine workers' rights. In Europe these are extensive, ranging from pension rights, the right to invalidity benefits, unemployment benefits, health insurance, and so on. All these key social rights were acquired during the last century. Giving them up is not easy.

The foreign labour market can be challenging and throw up some unexpected situations. You discover that you are not automatically entitled to the same number of days off or to proper health insurance. Working hours can be longer, childcare can be unaffordable or unavailable, your diploma may not be recognised.

Whether you are legal cohabitants or a married couple, legislation in your home country might offer you certain financial guarantees. Perhaps you can receive social security benefits from your government. Depending on your marriage agreement/cohabitation agreement, your partner may also be required to support you financially.

The law also guarantees certain rights upon the death of the expat. In this respect, an employer can offer certain benefits, or you can take out insurance.

What should you be mindful of?

Status – the expat's, and yours

What status does the expat's employer give to the partner? Are there any advantages for you, and can they be retained if you find work yourself? For example, if you sign a local contract, can you keep the expat's health insurance? If not, how can you replace it? What type of residence permit do you receive? If you want to work, under what conditions is that possible? What is the procedure if you want to work? Is your diploma recognised?

The website permitsfoundation.com lists information by country on work permits for expat partners. You can also find more information in Jennifer A. Patterson's *Financial Planning for Global Living* and Louise Wiles and Evelyn Simpson's *Thriving Abroad*. These books might not be tailored to your specific situation, but they do highlight potential pitfalls. Research is essential. For partners of diplomats, there are bilateral agreements between the country of origin and the country of destination. These specify the conditions under which partners with diplomatic status can work. The HR management of your Ministry of Foreign Affairs can offer you more information.

Married or not?

How did you get married? With or without a marriage agreement/ prenuptial agreement? Even if you do not have such an agreement, specific legal rights are laid down by law. Do your legal rights in marriage terms change if you move to another country? How long do you have to stay in that country?

Does the employer make a distinction between married and unmarried people? What are the terms if you are not married? Does the employer acknowledge a declaration of legal cohabitation? Does the host country make a distinction?

What are your terms/legal rights if you are legal cohabitants? If you have a declaration of legal cohabitation, you can sometimes sign a notarised contract with different terms to those set by the legislator. In some countries you will both need independent legal advice to do so.

What about divorce? What about custody of the children? Which laws are applicable? Those of the country of origin or the host country?

What about death? What benefits does your employer offer? Which legislation and inheritance tax applies – your home country's, or the host country's? Do you have life insurance cover? Is a will required?

The International Family Law Group LLP, a London-based law firm, has compiled a list aptly called 'Cupid's little legal checklist'. The list gives a good picture of what you should watch out for. Before departure you should seek independent advice from a lawyer specialised in international family law, preferably in the country of departure and in the proposed destination country.

cupid's little legal checklist

for moving abroad

1. Check your relationship is recognised in your destination country as there can be problems with e.g. same-sex marriage, civil partnership or cohabitation.
2. Check your visa status and whether you can reside in your destination country on a visa independent from your spouse or partner.
3. Check when moving with a child or planning to have a child in your destination country that your spouse or partner agrees on the circumstances and terms for you to return to your home country with the child, then record that agreement.
4. Check what your legal rights would be in your destination country if you were to separate or divorce whilst one or both of you lived there.
5. Check whether there is a gender bias in your destination country in respect of parental rights or financial rights upon separation or divorce.
6. Check how long you need to reside in your destination country before you or your spouse or partner can gain rights to start legal separation or divorce proceedings there.
7. Check you pack and carry with you any final family court orders, marriage certificates, divorce decrees, parental agreements and translations when you take a child from a country, as some border agencies require to see them.
8. Check whether any marital agreement/your marital regime is recognised in your destination country, or if you need to make a further nuptial agreement to comply with your destination's laws.
9. Check if you can open a bank account in your sole name in your destination country and in any event try to keep a sum of money aside for emergencies.
10. Check what legal rights you would be giving up by moving.

Cupid's little legal checklist, International Family Law Group LLP.

Don't be naive!

> *'If you leave me tomorrow Steph, what am I supposed to do? And if I want to leave you? (...) But you promised: you said, "My money is your money." You promised.'*

Don't be like Sophie, the main character in the novel *Indian Therapy* by Juliette Tissot. She failed to put any agreements in writing.

Expat partners can run into serious financial difficulties if their marriage breaks down and there are no agreements in writing. Uncertainties about alimony or living wages in the country of residence must be clarified. Sometimes this can result in a return to the home country. Expat partners with a different nationality from the expat, the so-called foreign-born spouses, should be particularly watchful of this.

When you know that a job contract abroad will never contain the same financial and social advantages as at home, you can look for alternatives to replace them first. This way you open up possibilities.

If you have solutions to the loss of legal guarantees, such as pension accrual, you can consider jobs that you might previously have ruled out. The options open to you to build up alternative securities depend on many factors: which country you go to, its legislation, what the employer offers, your status, your personal situation.

Take time to fully understand your rights that a marriage, labour or other contracts have given you. Be clear about the rights you don't want to give in. Then inform yourself how to keep them or how to replace them.

Sound legal advice is crucial. A visit to a lawyer or a notary will provide legal reassurance. Carefully prepare your questions, discuss them with your partner and do not forget about yourself. Sometimes the HR department of the employer can help you to get started.

Ask yourself a few questions

- What would you think about a job where you would have to pay for private health insurance to be adequately covered?
- Or a private pension savings fund?
- How does your partner feel about it?
- Does he/she want to support you financially? What agreements would you need to make in this regard?
- To marry or not to marry? What are the consequences of one or the other?
- What changes to the prenuptial or cohabitation agreement are needed?
- What agreements would you make in case of a divorce?

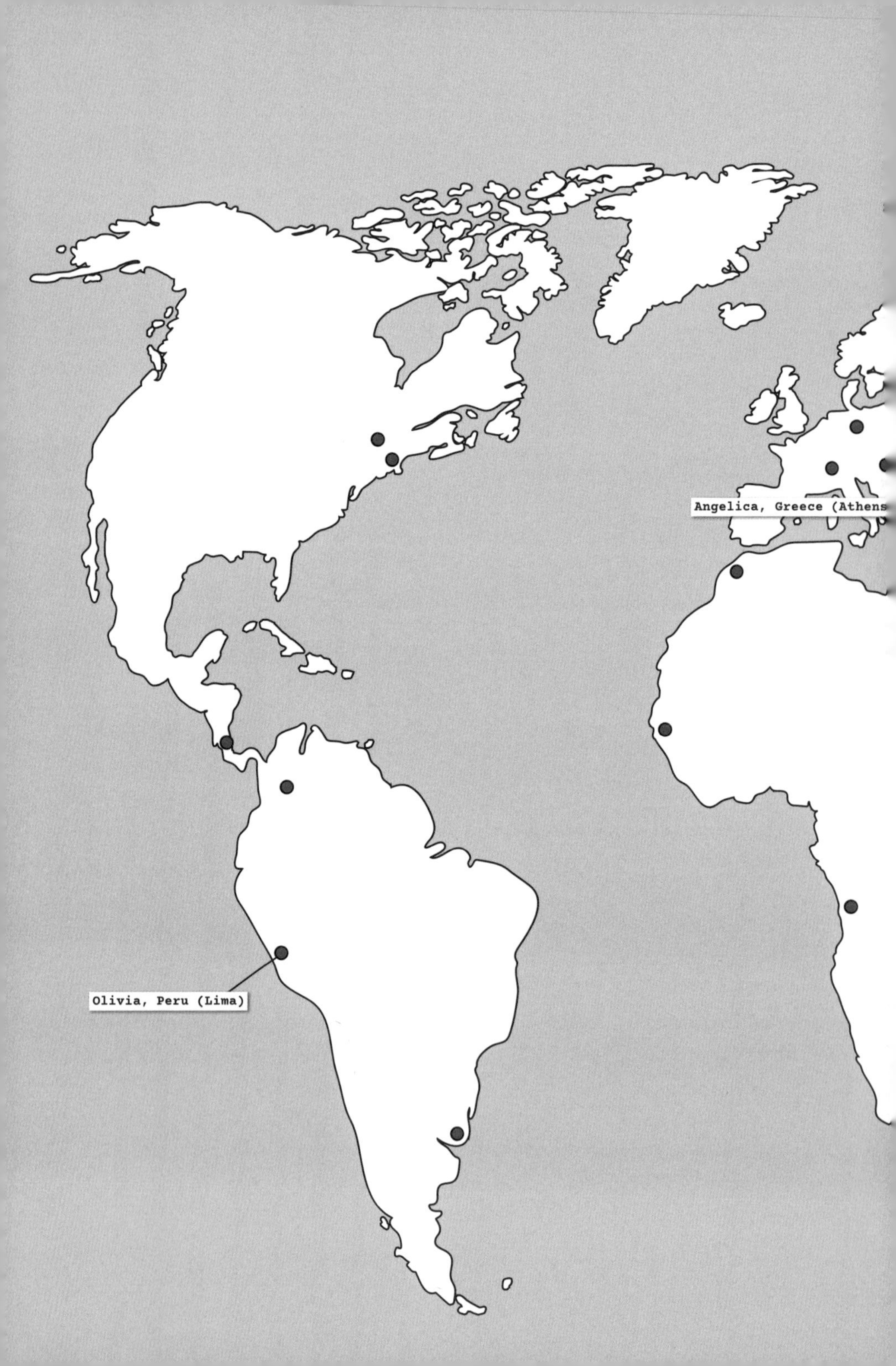
Angelica, Greece (Athens
Olivia, Peru (Lima)

– Stories from the field –

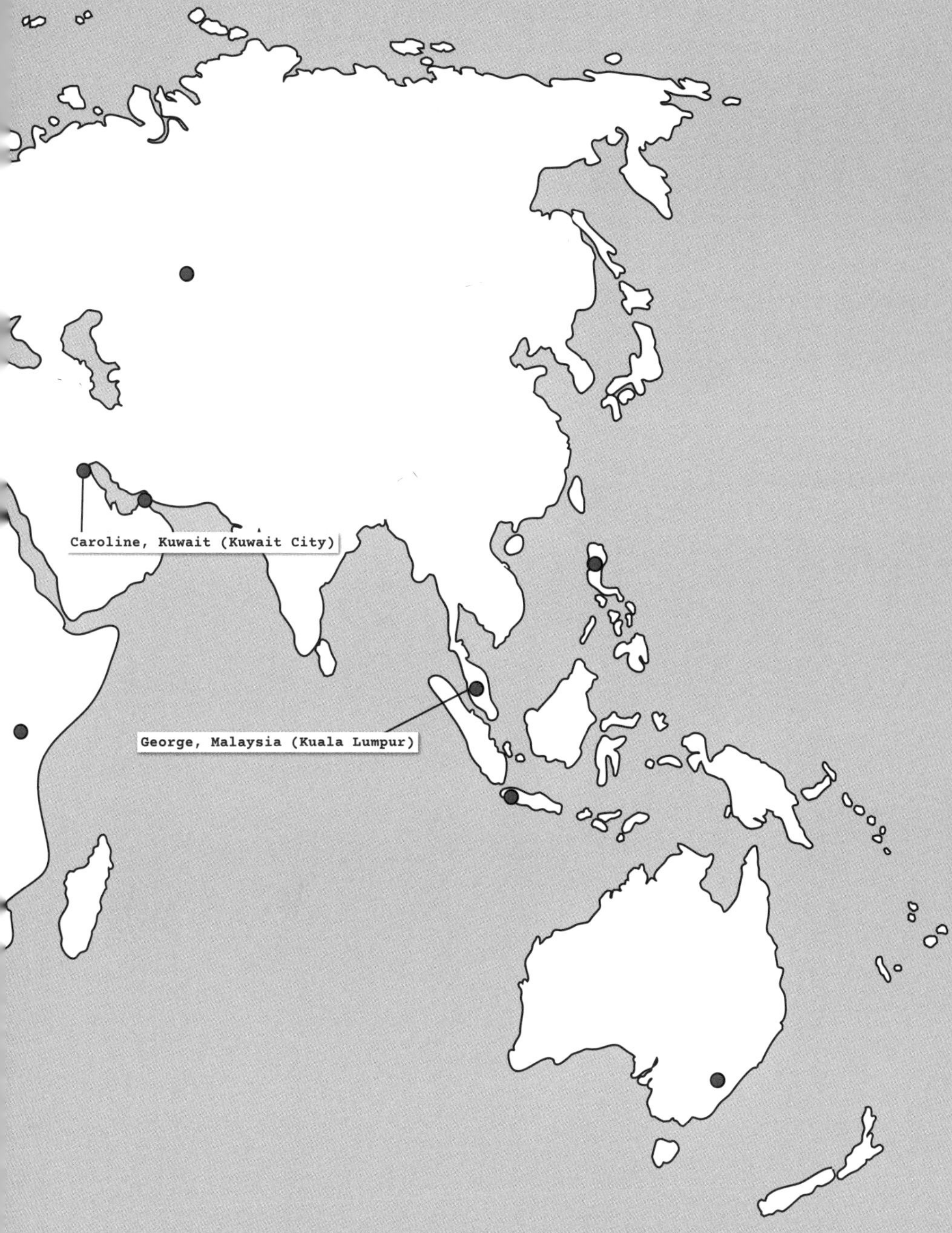

Olivia in Lima, Peru

Olivia is a graphic designer and teaches at a college of art. Her boyfriend Lucas is a development aid worker and is leaving for Peru for several years. She decides to go with him. As a teacher, she can take temporary unpaid leave and work on a self-employed basis. Olivia will shift her focus back to Design. She still has a number of legal matters to sort out. When starting her new business, Olivia discovers that the costs are high, as are the social charges. Even though she will undoubtedly earn little in the first few years, she takes out good health and pension insurance. She knows she will not make much money. Lucas agrees to contribute to the cost of her apartment. They decide to get married and, following a visit to the notary, opt for the additional benefits of a marriage agreement.

Olivia's choice focuses on the development of her professional skills. She wants to remain creative and seizes the opportunity to launch her own business. Now she can devote herself full-time to designing. In addition, she ensures that financial matters are covered.

George in Kuala Lumpur, Malaysia

George and Tina both have children from a previous marriage and one daughter, Rosalie, together. An international school in Kuala Lumpur makes Tina an attractive job offer and they make the move. George has many questions, both about his career and about the children. They both want their children to visit regularly and George's eldest son, Thomas, also wants to come along. But his mother is very reluctant. Will she still be able to see her son? And George wonders what would happen if his relationship with Tina ended. What about their daughter Rosalie? George and Tina need legal advice before taking a decision. They contact a lawyer specialised in international family law. The issues are set out in a legal agreement, and they can embark on their new adventure. Even Thomas's mother acquiesced.

This complex situation requires you to avoid burying your head in the sand, openly share your concerns with your partner, and seek expert legal advice.

Caroline in Kuwait City, Kuwait

Caroline works in the Finance department of a marketing company. She and her husband Theo, an engineer, are leaving for Kuwait. Because she does not have a work permit, she decides to pursue a PhD in financial sciences during the posting: it is a long-held dream of hers. Sometimes there are tensions in their marriage and a few of their friends are already divorced. Will their marriage survive a move abroad? Caroline feels vulnerable. Together they go to a notary and come to the conclusion that the best solution is to amend their marriage agreement. They also take out life insurance should Theo pass away. Caroline now feels more comfortable about giving up her work and accepts the challenge. She eagerly starts her studies.

Caroline pursues her dream. She contacts fellow students and other researchers. She mitigates the loss of salary and pension rights by amending the marriage agreement and taking out life insurance. In this way she will not be left out in the cold should the overseas adventure prove too much of a burden on their marriage.

Angelica in Athens, Greece

Angelica, a Filipino, meets Michael in her home country. She is so overjoyed that she soon decides to get married. After a few years, they leave for Spain and then Greece. Angelica makes friends quickly: she also befriends other Filipino women, one of whom is Teresita. Teresita describes the breakdown of her marriage, the particularly messy divorce and the ensuing difficulties concerning separation of assets. Angelica realises that she is unclear about her own situation. What if her marriage ended? What does Michael think? She dares not ask.

One evening, over a glass of wine, she voices her concerns to Michael. He understands how sensitive this is for Angelica. Moreover, he himself does not fully understand the ins and outs, so he suggests that they see a notary to discuss their situation and, if necessary, change their prenuptial agreement. Angelica is relieved.

The openness with which Angelica and Michael can talk about these problems strengthens the confidence they have in their marriage. It is not too late to settle financial matters that they overlooked when they first married.

Professional skills

'I always feel a certain resistance to getting out of my comfort zone, but afterwards, I'm so happy to have grown.' CARINE

'Always in for new things and challenges, I quickly say yes to opportunities. And doing so, my network grows.' MARIE

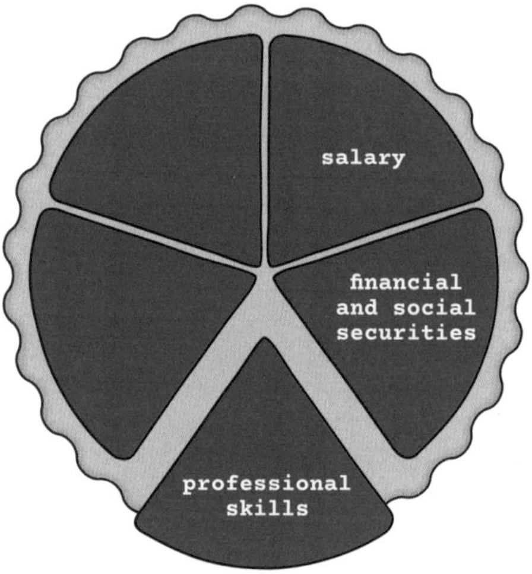

Lifelong learning

The skills you acquire at home and by interaction with your social environment and education are converted into productive work in a job. But your learning process does not stop there. When you work, you continue to develop professional skills, either in your area of expertise or in a totally different domain. If you stop working, so does your development, with a resultant loss of skills. The younger you are when you decide to give up your job and pack your bags, and the longer the period of inactivity, the greater the loss. The fear of losing professional skills is often great, and rightly so. Every employer checks your CV for the skills you have developed. If you fail to prove them, you will fall by the wayside during the selection process.

For expat partners who want to continue to develop professionally, giving up their job is a frightening prospect. After all, they assume that they will return to their home country at some point and, when they do, will want to rejoin the labour market. Professional skills are thus essential. For many expat partners, the challenge of remaining professionally active while simultaneously dealing with the challenges associated with moving abroad is demanding.

Keep your options open

There is a myriad of possibilities for developing and broadening your professional competencies. Expanding your options and thinking creatively are key. According to sociologist Stéphanie Talleux, 'moving abroad is an opportunity to identify and to acquire new skills. She talks about technical and relational skills, skills that are very personal, so that you can reinvent yourself again. She also emphasises the skills that are specific to an international environment: you can sharpen your language skills, learn about the local culture, and thus understand cultural differences and similarities.

Unless you can continue to pursue a conventional career, you will need to step out of your comfort zone. This requires courage, creativity, flexibility and perseverance, as well as the willingness to fail. It's not easy, but it can be done. Louise Wiles and Evelyn Simpson provide an overview of the options in *Thriving Abroad*:

- Find an opportunity to pursue your existing career in your new location.
- Identify a new career that you can develop in your new location.
- Review your skills and talents; look for a career that will fit, and be open to suggestions and experimentation. See what comes up and test it out.
- Seek to build a career or business that is portable and can move with you when you next relocate.
- Build a business locally.
- Embark on a new course of training and development as a basis for a new career move or to develop your knowledge and skills in your current professional area.
- Decide to see what shows up by getting out and networking in your local area.
- Look for voluntary work; this is often a good choice if you are not able for visa reasons to work in your current location.
- Consider developing a portfolio career – one that encompasses several of the suggestions above.

In their bestseller *A Career in Your Suitcase*, Jo Parfitt and Colleen Reichrath-Smith offer advice on how to achieve this. The book is also a good source if you want to fine-tune your CV or are invited to job interviews. The authors speak from personal experience. The watchwords are inventiveness and flexibility.

Voluntary work

Eva Hambach is director of the Flemish Support Centre for Voluntary Work and is active in international voluntary networks. She points out that voluntary work is not valued equally in all countries: 'In Belgium, employers don't attach the same importance to the skills gained in voluntary work as they do to those in paid work. It is different in the Anglo-Saxon world, where you can jump between voluntary and paid work without a loss of competence.' Voluntary work is an attractive professional option when abroad, especially in countries that do not issue work permits to the partner. But remain realistic about the cultural perception of voluntary work in your home country.

Your choice of voluntary work is critical. What are the priorities for you? Avoid getting carried away by projects that you do not want to be part of and are too time consuming. Voluntary work involves give and take. Do not feel guilty if you do voluntary work that also benefits you, for example if you learn important new skills or develop ones you already have.

Eva Hambach also points out how important it is to translate your competencies into the language of the employer. That in itself is a skill. Do not be tempted to downplay your voluntary work as 'something that you enjoy doing' during a conversation or job interview. Instead, present it as being equivalent to paid work, as an activity in which you 'developed teamwork skills, learnt to think in a solution-oriented way, led a team, etc'. Expat partners often have highly developed organisational and communication skills. They plan dinners, events and receptions for large groups. These soft skills are popular with employers. The clue is to start from the conviction that the absence of a salary does not make your job inferior, and to use the right management terms when talking about your personal skills, whether you gained them during voluntary work or not.

Patchwork career

Many expat partners choose not to work but instead make time for their family or their own personal development. This is no less valuable. It can also be the preferred option during a specific phase of life, before you become professionally active again. It goes without saying that you will not build up a conventional career during your period abroad. And yet there are many possibilities: exciting experiences are strung together over time, sometimes mutually connected, sometimes self-standing. This creates a patchwork career. While many jobs or activities might seem to have little in common, these experiences teach you skills that are useful when applying for a job when you return home. So be aware of the skills you develop: coordination, organisation, computer or logistics skills, etc. Do you think in terms of results and solutions? Do you like teamwork while remaining independent? Learn to list your skills: this is crucial in the job market.

Mobile career

You can also build a mobile career. You learn a profession that you can readily carry out anywhere: teacher, engineer, photographer, filmmaker, psychologist or coach. Perhaps, thanks to your current profession, you already have a sound basis for a mobile job. Or you have to change direction, or study again. Listen to the Tandem Nomads podcasts if you want to get started.

Tip: coaching
Consider a coach. Your job search may require a fair degree of professional help. Others can sometimes see what you do not. Why continue to struggle on your own if you can be guided professionally? At the end of the book, you will find websites of organisations that specialise in the various aspects of moving abroad. Many offer their services online.

Consider employment contracts that will allow you to develop professional skills beyond those in your field of expertise. This will improve your chances of finding a job abroad.

Creating a patchwork or mobile career increases your chances, not only abroad but also when you return to your home country.

When you work as a volunteer, you can develop (new) professional skills. Excluding voluntary work upfront limits your professional options.

Try out new experiences. A calculated risk or a well-considered career switch might benefit you personally and/or professionally. If necessary, have a coach assist you.

Ask yourself a few questions:

- If you do not find a job within your profession, in which other sectors are you willing to work? Under what conditions? Can you adapt those conditions to the circumstances?
- What retraining do you require?
- What added value will this bring when you return to the labour market in your home country?
- What new skills appeal to you? How can you develop these?
- If you do not find paid work, or you are not allowed to work, is voluntary work an option for you? If so, which type? Within or outside your field of expertise?
- What kind of voluntary work could offer you added value?

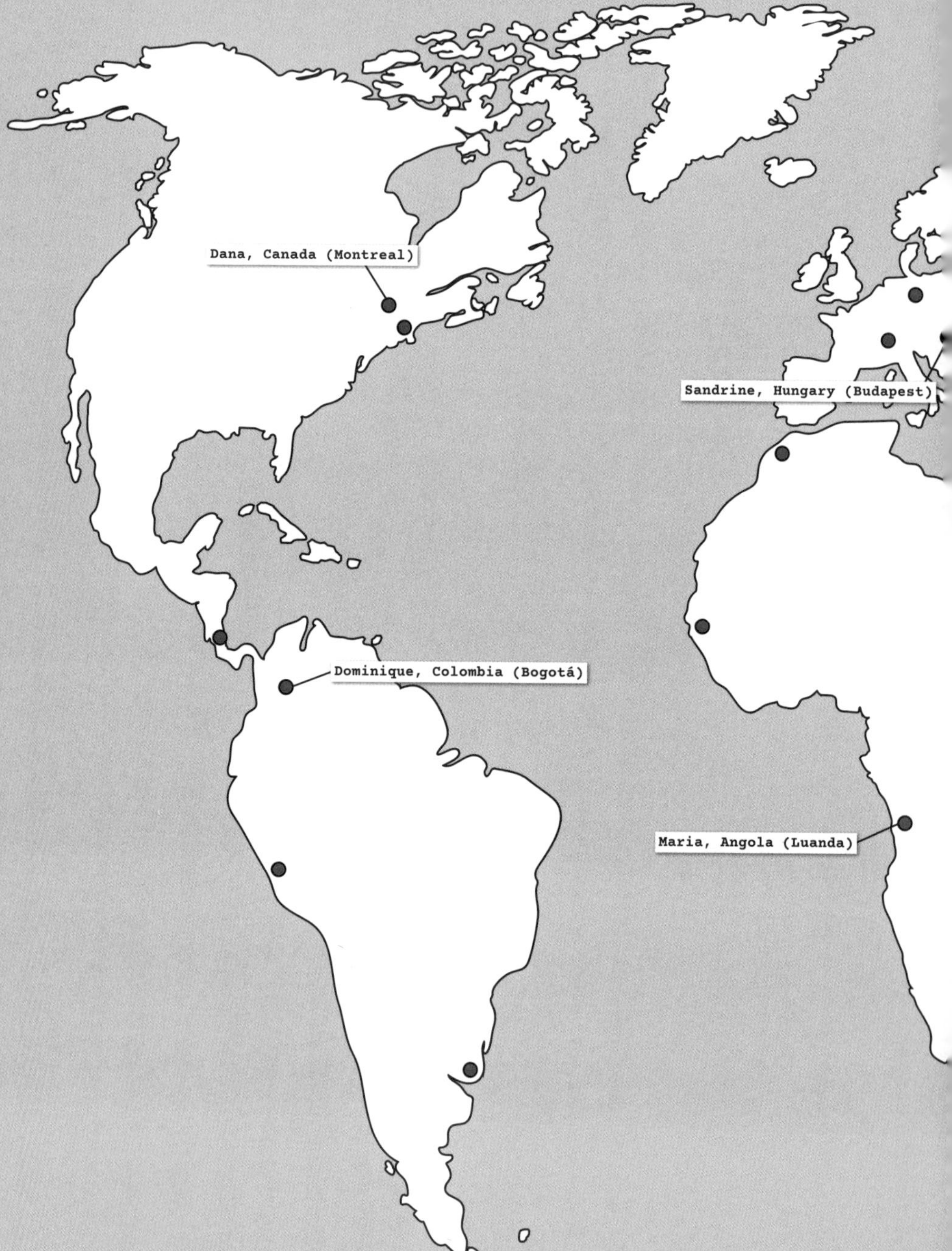

Dana, Canada (Montreal)
Sandrine, Hungary (Budapest)
Dominique, Colombia (Bogotá)
Maria, Angola (Luanda)

– Stories from the field –

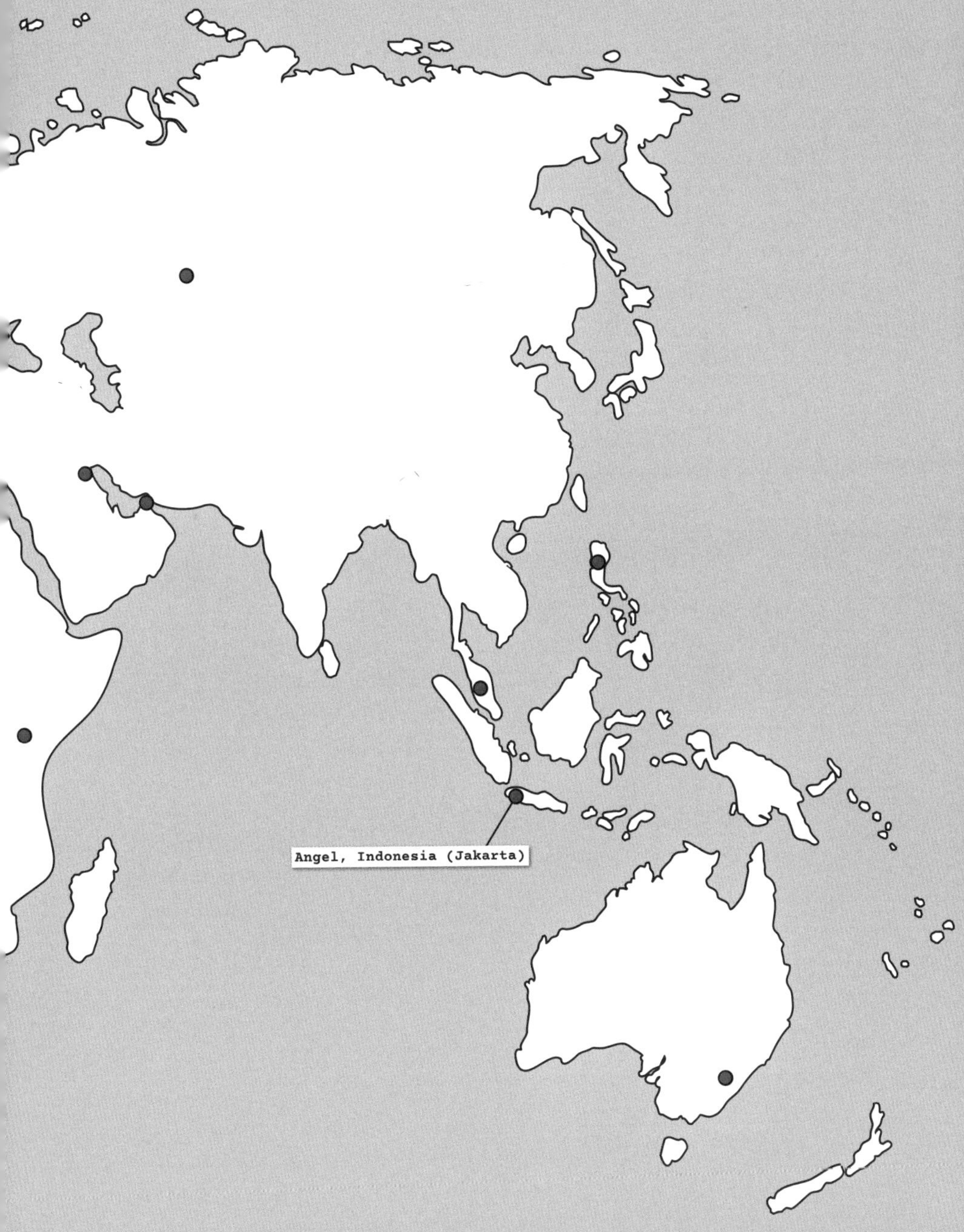

Maria in Luanda, Angola

Maria is a lawyer from Brazil. Law is one of the most challenging professions to take up abroad. When Maria is faced with the choice of whether or not to accompany her fiancé to Luanda, she hesitates: she is not familiar with Angolan law. But Maria has always been interested in IT as well as the financial sector. Through the UK's Open University, she studies an advanced master's programme. She does so because a company in Luanda offers her the chance to work in their accounting department. The job is part time and not that challenging but, combined with her studies, it allows Maria to embark on a new journey.

Maria develops professional skills that she will be able to use when she returns to her home country. Her legal background has given her a skill set that she can also use in the financial sector. Moreover, her studies give a real boost to her language skills.

Sandrine in Budapest, Hungary

Sandrine is a dentist and has a practice in Copenhagen, Denmark. She accompanies her husband Eric to Budapest. However, she would lose her license if she were to stop working as a dentist. To keep it, she needs a minimum number of patients. Sandrine therefore decides to keep a part-time practice in Copenhagen and join her husband for the rest of the time in Budapest. Living a totally separate life is not an option for her. She wants to go abroad and experience a new life.

The decision not to go full-time is not easy, but Sandrine's professional skills are a priority for her. She and her husband find a solution to the drop in her income: Eric gives her a contribution to compensate for it.

Angela in Jakarta, Indonesia

In her home country, Angela works as an administrative assistant. She enjoys her job and has pleasant colleagues. She is over the moon when, one evening, her husband announces that he is being transferred to Indonesia. She has become a keen yoga practitioner in her free time and sees the move to Jakarta as an opportunity to become a yoga teacher. Bidding farewell to her colleagues is hard but, at the same time, she looks forward to learning a new skill. She is fortunate to be able to take a career break for a few years.

Angela fully embraces the opportunity to turn her passion into a career and develop new professional skills. She does not know whether she will ever return to administrative work. Only time will tell.

Dominique in Bogotá, Colombia

On arrival in Bogotá Dominique, who is a teacher, opts for voluntary work. His wife often works long hours at the telecom company that employs her, and he wants to spend more time with their children. In a school in a poor neighbourhood, he sets up a multipurpose studio equipped with sewing machines and workbenches. This allows the disadvantaged children to discover their hidden talents. It's terra incognita for them – and for him. Before leaving for Colombia, Dominique and his wife had a marriage agreement drawn up to ensure that he would not suffer financially.

Through his voluntary work, Dominique learns new skills and competencies that could come in handy later in his career. He has never worked outside Europe and he finds working with Colombians fulfilling.

Dana in Montreal, Canada

Dana has moved to different countries eleven times. She has thoroughly enjoyed life in those exotic destinations while raising four children. Now she is back in Montreal, and all her children have left home. After so many years without a job, Dana does not believe that she can realistically return to the labour market. Through contacts, she joins a workshop for people looking for work. As a result, she finds work as a tour guide. The knowledge of languages she has gained during all the many years provides her with an extra asset.

Later, she comments: ‘It’s thanks to the coaching that I believed in myself again. The coach didn’t provide solutions, but taught me to look at myself differently so that I could find them for myself. It has put me back on track. I don’t earn much, but it’s my money. I am so proud, and I notice that my children and husband are also proud of me.’

Social life and structure

'Forcing myself out of the house remains both a challenge and a necessity.' CARINE

'Without people I don't function. They give me energy to act.' MARIE

The fixed structure is lost

'Work' contributes to the fixed structure of the day or week. You go to work, perform specific tasks, interact with your colleagues, and go home. It is not always up to you how you fill your working day. That structure is an asset. If you have to give up work in order to go abroad, the physical move itself will keep you busy. But once that is complete, you suddenly have the luxury of time. If you have no children, not only is there no compelling reason – this may sound harsh – to get up in the morning, but there is also no-one to talk to. No colleagues with whom to discuss the latest television programme, no bosses to report to and no team to share your plans with. And even if you have children, the day can be quite lonely without like-minded grown-ups. How do you get through the day? The question can be scary. Loneliness lurks around the corner. If you want to establish friendships and see more than just the interior walls of your house, you are going to have to take the initiative, in a new country and often in a different language.

The difference with the expat

Initially there is a significant difference between the rhythm of life of the expat and that of the partner. After all, their situations are quite different. The expat has a specific job function in an office or other workplace, with colleagues who show him/her the way, and responsibilities that can often be challenging. At first, the expat will need to familiarise himself/herself, and work long hours as well as go on business trips. The partner who previously worked but is now housebound in a foreign country, with or without children, also faces significant changes. The high pace of life of the busy expat is often in stark contrast to the slow ticking of the clock for the partner. But that can change over time.

The great social earthquake

A new social circle

It goes without saying that working outside the home brings social contacts: you interact with colleagues, customers, suppliers, etc. These relationships are of a very different nature to those with friends, family or neighbours. They are important to our daily lives but often taken for granted. You will only miss them when they are gone. And even though you can easily keep in touch via WhatsApp, Skype and a plethora of other means of communication, friends, family and colleagues are not physically present: just dropping by or meeting up is no longer an option. As 'partner of', your social relationships are genuinely shaken up. How do you fill the vacuum? Perhaps the many networking events that are organised in the expat community will generate new social contacts. Are those enough for you? Or do you want to start your own new social circle? Anne Copeland's research from the Interchange Institute shows that women with local friends (strong or casual) adapt best. Those who rely mainly on long-distance contacts, including via email or WhatsApp, face the biggest adjustment.

Integration

Work has an important social function: it has become the main vehicle for inclusion in society. Those without a job quickly feel excluded. The classic working model – nine to five in an office – is no longer the rule. In the post-industrial world, work has become more flexible, for employer and employee alike. Today, work has many formats: flexible hours, working from home, part-time work, and career breaks. Employment conditions have also changed: the distinction between work time and leisure time is more striking; periods of unemployment occur, etc. These changes, together with the possibilities offered by IT, give you more mobility in the job market and allow your career to follow many paths. These developments are a real asset for expat partners: they increase the possibility to work. Thanks to the Internet, you can continue to work for your previous employer – or a new one – back home from your new base abroad. Indeed, working from home, which does not require as much local integration, enhances the sense of belonging: after all, pursuing a profession is often considered as being 'integrated' in a broader social context.

Get out of the house and start networking!

The good news is that you can compensate for the loss of your work contacts and the fixed structure a job offers. To do so, you need to take the initiative, get out of your comfort zone and start looking. There might well be activities that you have always wanted to do, but never had the time for: social or sports activities, piano or drawing lessons, dance, or a creative writing course, and so on. 'Just do it' should be your motto. You have to take steps to reorganise your own time. Whether you decide to do a job over the Internet, work from home or stop working altogether, you will still need to leave the house to meet people. In most countries, there are associations to help newcomers. Ask your partner's colleagues. You can also seek help through Facebook groups for expats: you will immediately receive numerous tips.

Your new network might even lead to a new job. It is an excellent way to find work, as evidenced by statistics from the Expat Value survey:

» 81% find work via a network (physical rather online);
» 30% through spontaneous applications;
» 15% by responding to vacancies;
» 4% via headhunters.

(The total is higher than 100% because multiple answers were possible in the survey.)

'These jobs are snatched up by people who are not necessarily better qualified than you,' says Jo Parfitt in *A Career in Your Suitcase*, 'but who are better connected.' There is a wide range of courses that will teach you how to improve your networking skills. Jo and Colleen give helpful advice on local and online networking, clubs and associations, and the skills that you can develop to improve yourself.

Why not start your own network? Like-minded people in your new country can often be a big help with your integration. Find role models, people who, like you, want to stay active. Learn from their experience. Social groups online can also be inspirational, select what is useful for you. Share your own expertise. That way you can become a model for others.

If, as an expat partner, you look for work with the same daily or weekly schedule as in your home country, and with the same type of work relationships, you will limit the possibilities. Be open to other options and look for solutions when your initial expectations are not met.

If working 'away from home' is essential for your social integration and a traditional full-time career is not possible, consider other forms of work: part-time work, voluntary work, self-employment or retraining.

If working from home, online work or not working for a while is an option for you, establish new contacts in other ways.

Either way, start your network and discuss with your partner how you can achieve a new balance given the difference in the rhythm of your life and his/hers. Consciously plan your own daily and weekly schedule.

Ask yourself a few questions

» Do you want to work 'away from home' or is working from home an option?

» If you decide to work from home, what are the logistics of doing so in your new house?

» Can you get a work-at-home position with your current employer? Or with another company?

» What options do you have regarding setting up your own business?

» Can you see yourself in a position with little human contact? In your spare time, can you make up for the loss of social contact at work?

» What skills do you have that would help you build your new social network? What kind of coaching can help you achieve this?

» What arrangements do you need to make with your partner and/or your children so that you have time and space for your activities/work?

» How do you organise your own daily routine? How can you improve it?

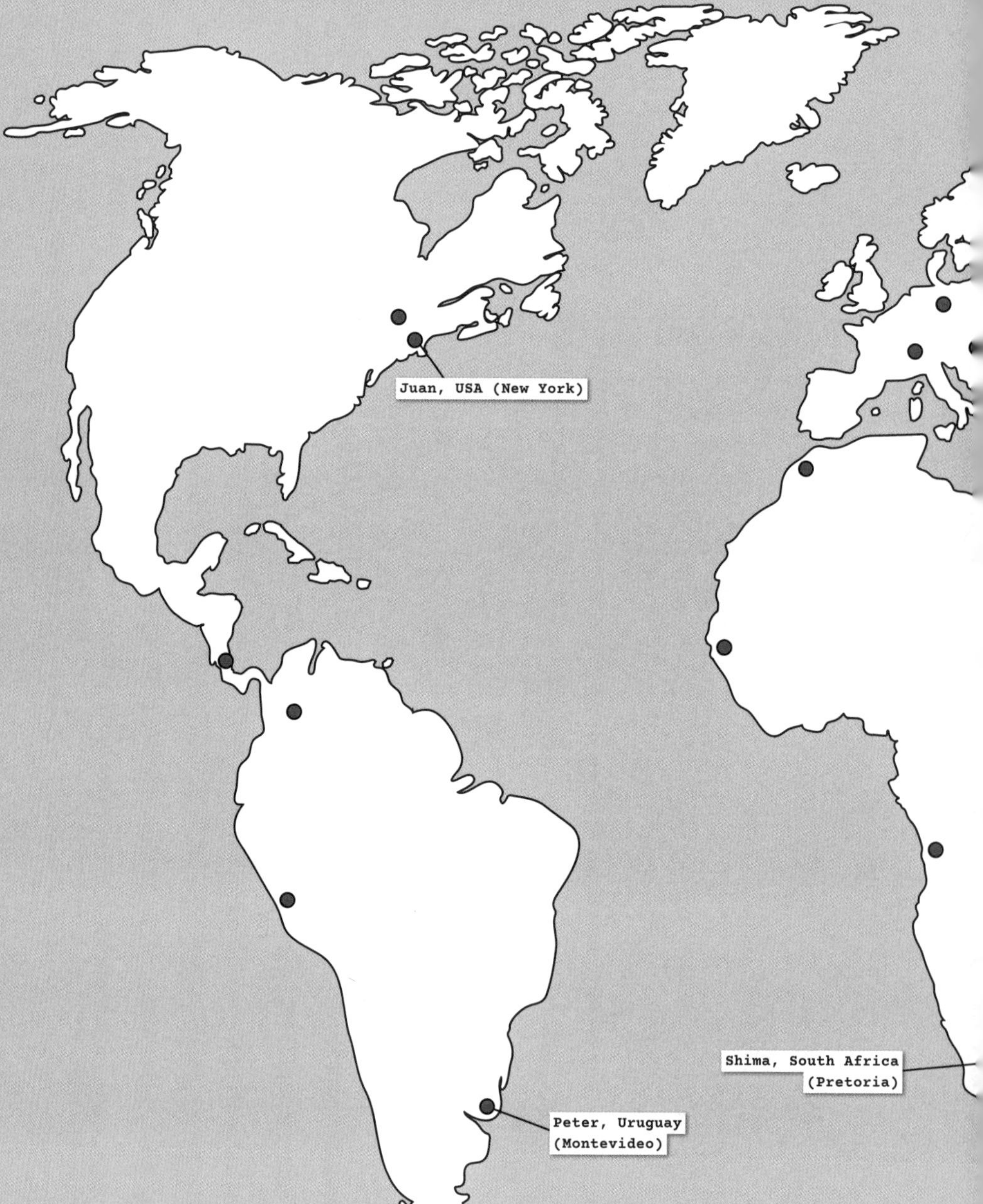
Juan, USA (New York)
Shima, South Africa (Pretoria)
Peter, Uruguay (Montevideo)

— Stories from the field —

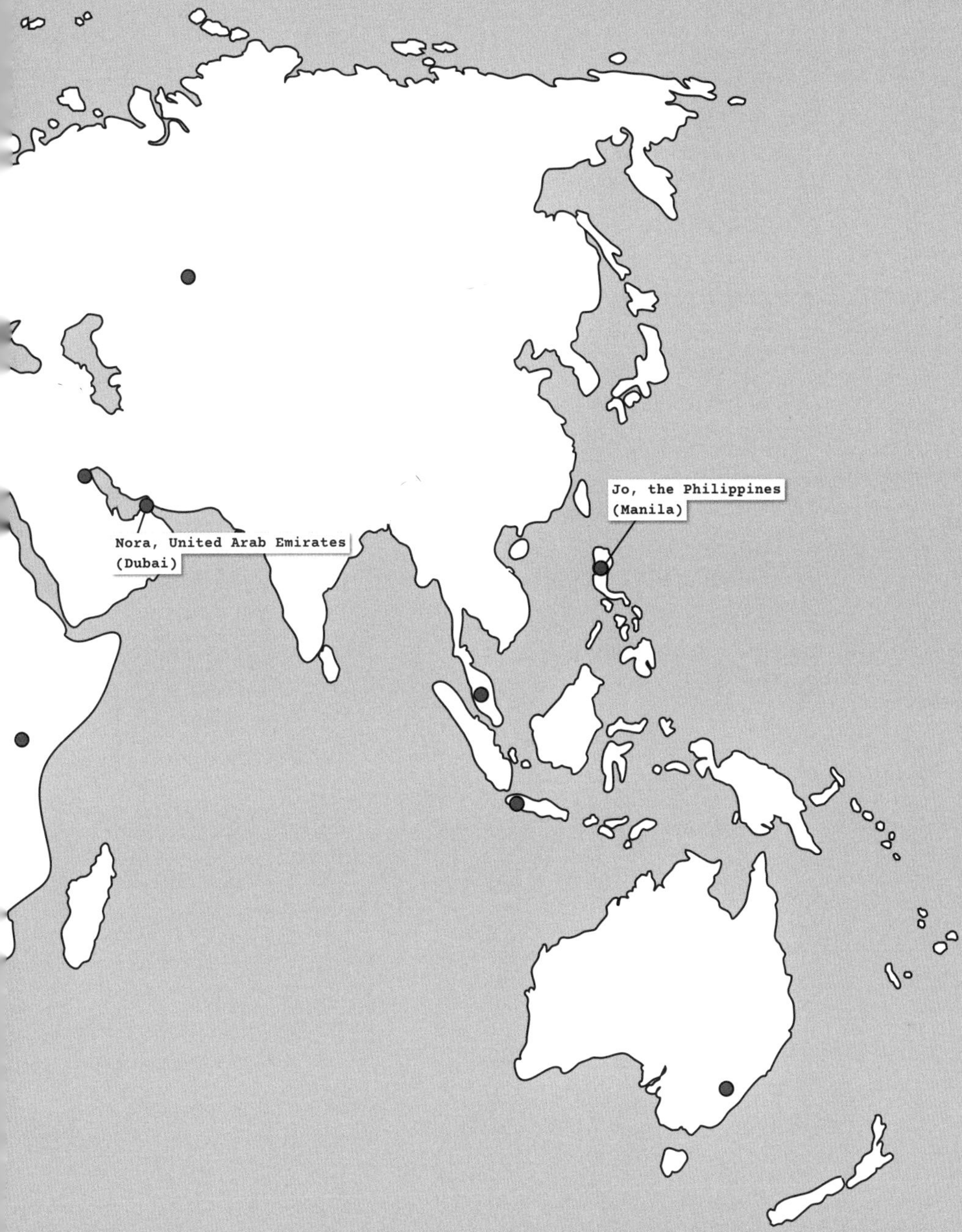

Nora in Dubai, United Arab Emirates

Nora works as an engineer for a large international company. She loves her job and is very sociable. When her husband lands a job in Dubai, Nora's employer has no objection to her going too. For the most part, she will be able to work from home. The company also pays for a ticket for her to fly back when necessary. Nora is delighted, but also anxious. Home alone all day behind the computer? That can be very lonely. A Facebook group of expats in Dubai reveals that there is a busy social life. So she decides to accompany her husband. On arrival, she joins some expat groups, registers at a fitness club and starts singing in a choir again.

For Nora, giving up her job is not an option, but she is fortunate that she can continue by working from home. She makes up for the absence of work colleagues by making friends in her spare time.

Jo in Manila, the Philippines

Jo is a civil servant in the Ministry of Defence in New Zealand. When he decides to accompany his life partner Oliver to Manila, he takes a career break. But this leaves him feeling bored. Every day is the same and he misses his colleagues. Jo is passionate about film. He meets several local artists. He soon sets up a workshop and, after a few months, he becomes a photography and film teacher. He teaches twice a week. The artists do not have the money to pay him. But this is not an issue for Jo. He has an agreement with Oliver about how to share the income. Jo also goes to the gym and takes tennis lessons.

Through voluntary work, Jo learns to work with people from a different culture. Teaching is also a new professional skill. Now his week is well structured.

Shima in Pretoria, South Africa

Before her departure from Senegal, Shima worked in the HR department of a media production company in Dakar. On arrival in Pretoria, she starts her own online company for the import and export of Senegalese products. It is not easy to get it off the ground and she spends a lot of time on the computer. She notices that being at home makes her feel lonely and that she is not getting enough exercise. She joins a jogging club, but not much talking is done and Shima needs more social contact. She meets plenty of new people through the International Spouses Association and enjoys the twice-monthly meetings at which she can chat with others in a similar position. But it puts pressure on her work, so she decides to limit participation to once a month. This achieves the balance she seeks.

Shima opts to set up her own company. Her need for social contacts forces her to take initiative to meet people, even when it costs time. Meeting people gives Shima the extra energy she needs to deal with her business.

Juan in New York, USA

While on holiday in New York, Juan meets Carmen, a young diplomat. It is love at first sight. But Juan has just started his own catering company back home in Argentina. He is not prepared to give that up. So instead he regularly flies to New York and back. When he is in New York, he monitors the daily routine of his catering business via webcam and Skype. That works well. But Carmen has long working hours. Juan often feels lonely at Carmen's place with just his computer for company. At an expat party, Juan meets Denis, who is a gardening volunteer in Central Park. That appeals to Juan: he misses exercise and nature, and it also gives him the chance to get to meet more New Yorkers. He commits himself to two mornings a week.

For Juan, choosing to give up his work for a budding relationship is too difficult. But he visits Carmen regularly. Through inventiveness and flexibility he buys time and he remains financially independent. He commits himself socially in his free time.

Peter in Montevideo, Uruguay

Peter decides to accompany his wife Louise to Montevideo when she is offered a job in the hotel sector. He has a great deal of experience in policy management with NGOs and is confident that he will find work quickly. This proves harder than he initially imagined, but he refuses to give up. He accompanies Louise to social events to promote the hotel. There he grabs the opportunity to tell people that that he is looking for work and is taking intensive Spanish lessons. He volunteers at a local NGO in order to get out of the daily routine at home. He gradually gains a clearer picture of what the labour market has to offer. Applying for a job is lonely and time-consuming. It takes eight months before he gets lucky. There is a vacancy at an NGO that collaborates with the one where Peter works. Peter applies for the job and, thanks to his experience and excellent network, he is hired. He frequently has to travel throughout Uruguay. After a while, Louise says, 'Peter sees much more of the country than I do.'

Peter uses expat contacts and his voluntary work to build his own network. That way he continues to work on his profile. Thanks to his perseverance, he manages to find a paid job.

Identity

'Once you're out of the labour market, you simply cease to exist.'
'I have nothing.'
'I am nothing. My career filled my life. Now the abyss.'
'The feeling of being air. They look right through you.'

EXPAT COMPANIONS

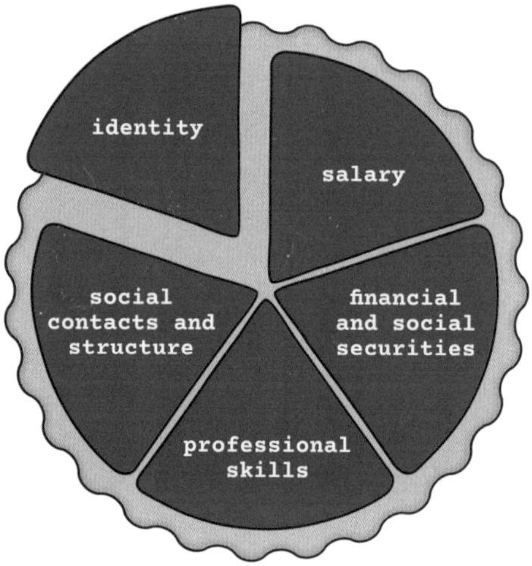

Who are you? What do you do?

'Who are you?' – or, more often, 'What do you do?' – are frequently asked questions when you are in a new environment. If you continue to live in the same place, people know you. They know who you are, and questions such as 'Who are you?' and 'What do you do?' are infrequent. These questions are sensitive for an expat partner. You give up work, move with your partner, and end up in a new environment. You are abroad because your partner found work there, and your children go to school there. Quickly you become 'partner of' or 'parent of'. Expat partners often struggle with the question: 'What's left of me?'. You are constantly introducing yourself to people you have never met before. If you are a woman you even lose your name: you suddenly become 'Mrs Peter Jones'. Yet male expat partners keep their own name. 'Mr Charlotte Jones' is simply not done. What discrimination!

If the lines between the professional identity of the expat and yourself become blurred, this can accentuate the crisis of identity. You are presented as Anna, the wife of the ambassador, or Joanne, the wife of the CEO of Company X. Robin Pascoe, an expat expert and author of A *Moveable Marriage*, expresses this beautifully: 'So what's a spouse to do to combat the shock of being known as Mrs Husband's Job ...?' . The danger is that you too will start seeing yourself as an extension of the expat's professional identity if others do so. And this can lead to a feeling of loss of identity.

What about male expat partners?

Men tend to derive their identity from their job more so than women. Does going abroad as a male expat partner represent a greater challenge? Most male partners work (full-time, part-time, from home, etc.) or look for work. Males make up 10% of all expat partners, so they are a small group. But not just expat partners struggle with a new reality. During the opening of an exhibition at a Western embassy in Kinshasa, you could hear a pin drop when...

With a group of invited guests, Carine is standing next to the curator of an exhibition, who introduces them to the artist. He proceeds, 'I would like to introduce you to Mr Franc, who is CEO of bank X, and his wife, Clara. This is Mrs Heller, the ambassador of Germany; this is Carine, the wife of the EU ambassador; and this is Mrs Clark, manager of a telecom company; and this is Louis, er, ehm... a good friend.' Louis is Mrs Clark's husband. The curator does not introduce the man as 'husband of', as he did with the wife of the bank manager and Carine. He does not know what to do because Louis is a man, and this seems to pose a problem to him. Then the ambassador of Germany whispers in Carine's ear: 'We really could do with that book of yours.' She, too, noticed the uncomfortable situation.

Who is Louis in society? Has he lost his identity? How does he define himself? And how would you introduce the male partner of an expat? Do you do it in a different way to female partners?

What defines us?

Nobody has said it better than the American Christopher O'Shaughnessy in *Arrivals, Departures and Adventures In-Between*. He lived, worked or travelled in more than a hundred different countries and is a gifted speaker at international forums on topics such as globalisation and cross-cultural communities. He wonders what defines us: 'So, odd noises aside, what does define us? What describes us? Is it our beliefs, customs, and the way we think and behave? Is it our language, likes, tastes, passions, and talents? Is it our history, nationality, worldview, and surroundings? Probably. That's what makes identity such an endeavour to figure out. It's messy, complicated and ultimately quite beautiful.'

Many have pondered the question 'What is an identity?'. Expat experts Debra R. Bryson and Charise M. Hoge carried out important social work on this theme with expat families in Bangkok. In their book

A Portable Identity, they describe identity based on four core facets. If you analyse each aspect in depth, you end up with a thorough self-study. The authors offer you step-by-step tools to find your way during your life abroad. We will briefly discuss the four facets.

» **First, there is the internal view of yourself.** This includes your perceptions of yourself, what you believe, your values and attitudes, your likes and your dislikes, your gender and your body image.
» **The second facet that in part makes up your identity is how external factors affect you.** How do others – family, friends, acquaintances, colleagues – see you? Which societal influences have an effect on you? How is your interaction with the community you live in and are involved with? What is the impact of the culture in which you live?
» **The third facet consists of the roles you occupy.** Roles help you determine who you are and what you do. You start out as a child. Whose child? Firstborn or not? Girl or boy? Are you a sister or brother, parent, friend, student, colleague or neighbour? These roles bring culturally determined expectations and rules for interpreting and assessing behaviour. Your self-esteem is affected by the roles you play.
» **The fourth facet encompasses the important relationships that you have with others.** Who are the most important people in your life? How meaningful are those relationships to you? And how did those relationships help determine who you are today?

Your life, and thus your identity, is constantly evolving. It is often said that people change. Identity is not static, certainly not for someone moving to another country. Events you experience have an impact – big or small – on who you are. If your job is taken away or changes significantly, facets that are part of your identity will change. In this way your self-image can change and the value you attach to your career and professional environment.

Moreover, the new image that your friends, family and colleagues have of you now that you are unemployed, or a housewife/ househusband, can also influence you. Your status within society is evolving: your integration into your new community presents you with new roles. And with those roles come different expectations. New relationships that you build and those you leave behind also make a mark on who you are.

There are so many facets that determine your identity. Which are important to you but have nothing to do with your profession? Do this exercise and find answers to the following questions without mentioning your occupation or anything related to it.

» Which characteristics and adjectives would you use to describe yourself?
» How do you see yourself in your new situation?
» What do you believe? Which values and attitudes are important to you?
» What do you like?
» How do others perceive you, both at the previous and new places of residence? Is their opinion important to you?
» What is your place in both your previous and new community? Do you feel included? Or are you sidelined?
» What impact does your own culture have on you? And the new culture in which you live?
» Which roles do you fulfil? Have new ones been added? What do you expect from these? What does your environment expect?
» Has your confidence changed? In what sense?

All your answers represent building blocks for your identity.

'Identity' is a complex notion

If you identify yourself strongly with your profession and you suddenly stop working, you face a greater challenge. By seeing all facets of your identity, you broaden your perspective and you can find alternative answers to the questions 'What do you do?' and 'Who are you?'. If you were a doctor before you went abroad, do you still say, 'I am a doctor'? Or do you state some of the other facets of your identity when the question arises, or other activities that you now follow? Does your profession disappear from your identity list if you no longer pursue it, or will it remain part of you? And how will this change over time? Will your previous profession no longer be a part of who you are in ten or twenty years' time?

Seize the opportunity!

Here too the golden rule applies: get out of the house and start networking! You are at a party and you need to introduce yourself. This is an opportunity. If you are looking for work, say so, and immediately add what kind of work you are looking for. Do not restrict yourself to a particular sector: keep your options open. At expat parties, there is a fair chance that you will meet people from many different walks of life. Your network is the most effective vehicle for landing a job. We emphasised this in Chapter 4. Arm yourself against empty gazes for you are sure to encounter them. Instead, focus on the people who are open to your story.

If you are not looking for work, talk about other aspects that help determine your identity. Consciously choose those that you like to talk about and that most fascinate you. Highlight one aspect, then pick another, as long as it does not feel too self-centered and remains interesting for you and your conversation partner.

Madame la Charité

For many of us, being of value in society is a component of who we are. You cannot be disconnected from your environment. You are part of it, and you want to contribute to it. 'Being of value' is often achieved through the job you do but, consciously or unconsicouly you do so much more to feel useful. The value attached to it can vary significantly from person to person. The loss of a job can also have a major impact. The feeling of being useless can harm your personal and social identity. How do you compensate for this?

It is a cliché that expat partners often work with charities. Half a century ago this was generally the case. This is nothing to sneer at. These days several expat partners feel the need to be of use to society. That kind of work can be to your advantage. Gaëlle Goutain and Adélaïde Russell confirm this in *Conjoint Expatrié: Réussissez votre séjour à l'étranger*: 'The sense of being socially useful is especially strong through voluntary work if you position yourself in a dynamic of contributing: contributing time as well as skills. You must allow yourself to evaluate what you get out of it. A win-win situation is best. You win something, and so does the other person.'

What you do, determines who you are. If your job occupies a large portion of the spectrum of elements from which you build your identity, losing it has a greater impact. But you do and are so much more.

By viewing the entire spectrum of your 'identity', you broaden your perspective. If you regard your profession as one of the aspects of your identity, you will be able to identify the others. They too determine your identity. This will allow you to benefit from these other aspects. You shift your focus. You can adjust your self-image and discover other professions or cultivate activities that also contribute to who you are. This allows you to grow.

Ask yourself a few questions:

- How important is your profession to your identity? How can you redefine this aspect of your identity?
- What, outside your profession, is important to you?
- How can you introduce yourself without mentioning your profession? Or without mentioning the job of your partner, the expat?
- Can you identify with another activity? Another profession? With other competencies?
- What questions do you ask someone you have just met?
- How does your culture view a working mother, a non-working woman, or a man who gives up his job to accompany his wife abroad? Do you conform to the norms of your community, or do you fall outside their scope?
- How has your status changed as a result of your move abroad?
- Who are the significant people in your life? How do they view your new life? What effect do their opinions have on you?

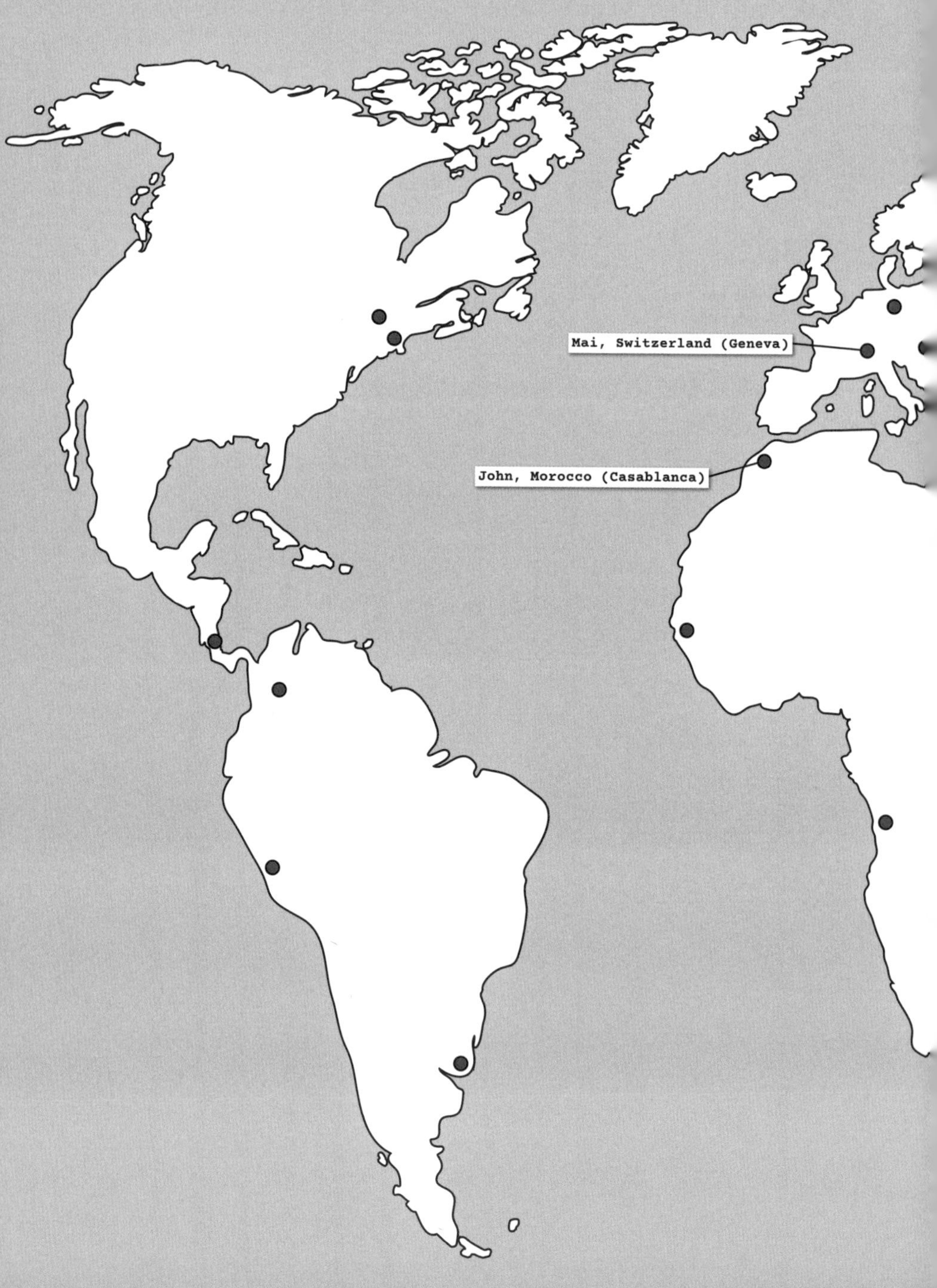

Mai, Switzerland (Geneva)
John, Morocco (Casablanca)

– Stories from the field –

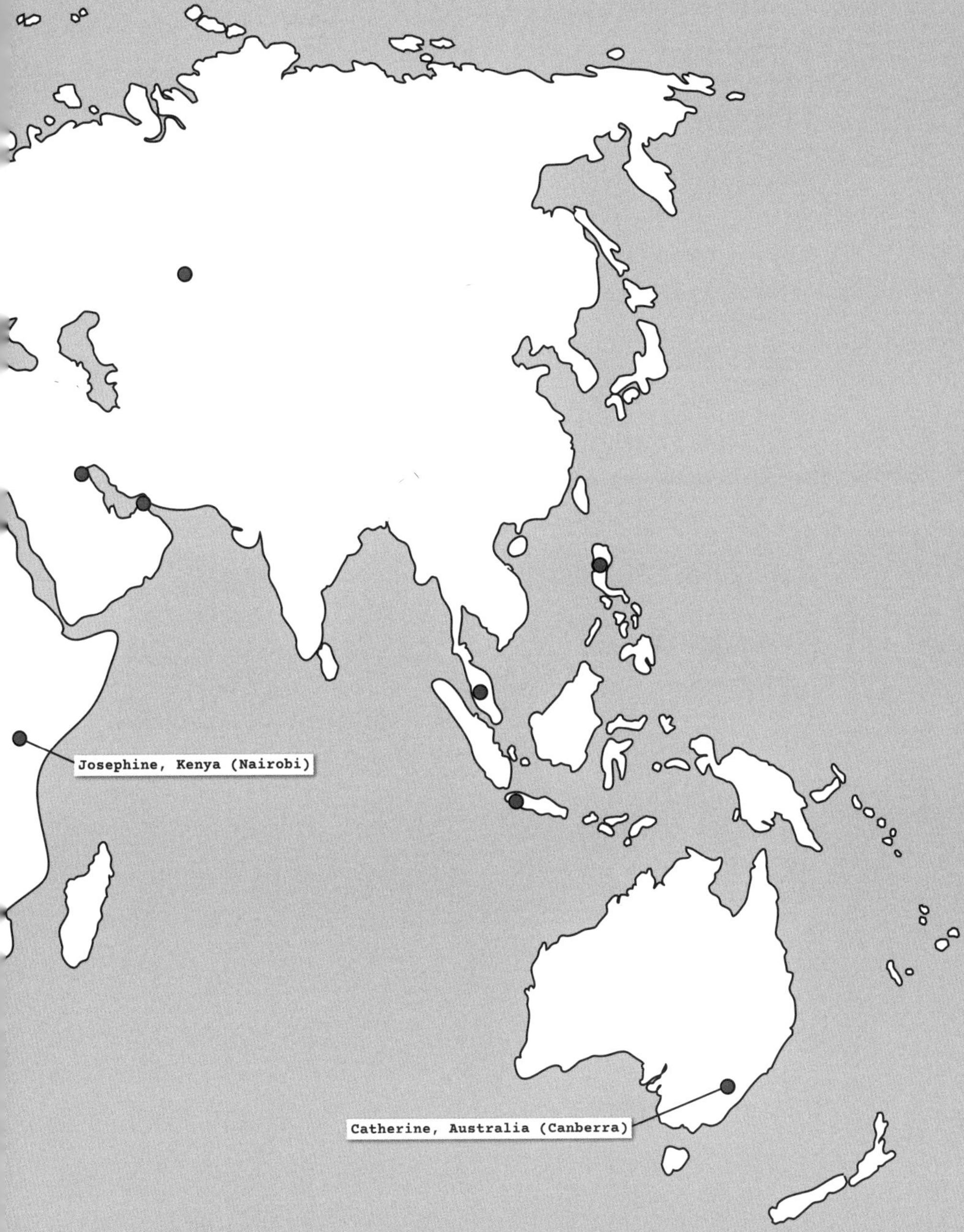

An anonymous source in *Conjoint Expatrié* by Gaëlle Goutain and Adélaïde Russell:
I feel like 'me': unique, one-of-a-kind, and at the same time rich and complex because of everything that defines me: my body and my mind, my gender, my personality, my traits, my feelings and emotions, my conscience, my subconscious, my thoughts, my values, my beliefs, my appearance, my needs, my desires, my motivation, my taste, my attitude, my skills, my abilities, my limits, my social and professional function, my roles (family, community, work), my status, my life project, my relationships, my cultural references, my faith, my family and cross-generational history.

Here we see that identity stems from individually related and socially related matters. These two 'orders' are indivisible because they interact, according to Goutain and Russell.

Mai in Geneva, Switzerland
Mai lives with her husband in Geneva. She met him at the hospital in Lubumbashi, Democratic Republic of Congo, where she worked as a doctor in the emergency department. After marrying, they moved to Europe and Mai stopped work. It was not easy. Her degree is not recognised and she feels useless. In her neighbourhood, there is a nursing home that is looking for new staff. Mai is interviewed and agrees to work for a few weeks initially as a volunteer on a trial basis. After the trial period, she is so enthusiastic that she does not mind no longer being able to work as a doctor. She goes on a short training course and joins the care home full-time.

Working, surrounded by colleagues, and feeling useful to society are important to Mai. She accepts that she no longer has the status of a doctor. Going back to medical school is too difficult for her. She wants a short-term solution. By launching a new career, Mai gives a fresh perspective to her identity.

Catherine in Canberra, Australia

'I want to belong again. If you don't work anymore, you don't belong anymore.' While Catherine is expressing her distress, she is at home and has been chatting with her best friend on the other side of the world for hours via WhatsApp. After ten years abroad, she is back in Canberra. Her husband, a diplomat, commutes to work every day. The children cycle to school. And Catherine? She is at home. All her friends and acquaintances have paid jobs: they live in dual-income households. The other parents at school also work. With whom can she share her experiences, or do something, during the day? When she does meet people, she always gets the question 'So what do you do?'. She finds it difficult to regard herself as a housewife. Abroad, she did not have a problem with it, because there was so much that was new to discover. Catherine was a journalist before her move abroad. She does not want to return to the profession: too much has changed. She learnt to cook exotic dishes abroad. Home cooking has always been a passion. The solution? Establish a small company as a private chef. It takes a lot of effort, but she feels alive again. She also notices that her children look at her differently. They never expected that: mummy starting her own business! She appreciates their proud looks.

Catherine feels isolated and alienated when she returns to her home country. She struggles with who she is. Through her experience abroad, she identifies a profession that helps her to build a new identity. She is delighted to be active in the job market again.

John in Casablanca, Morocco

John is a manager in a consultancy company. His wife lands an excellent job in the hotel sector in Casablanca. John wants to accompany her. His job has been a challenge, and he feels it is time for something new. However, sitting at home and walking the dog every day is not enough. He feels a profound sense of emptiness. How will he fill his day? Who is he now? The 'husband of'! Through his wife's network, John meets young people who are starting a business. They face problems with business plans, financing, staff, etc. John has a lot of experience and offers them advice. He does not ask for payment. But he feels fulfilled. The project is growing. He has more ideas. He launches a website through which he obtains paid assignments and makes podcasts. And he starts to put his thoughts in writing. A book! From manager, to consultant, to writer!

At first, John's career is over when he moves abroad. It was a conscious decision, but he nonetheless feels an emptiness. He does some research and slowly sees a clear path ahead. The skills from his first career set him on the road to building a second career, one that connects nicely with his wife's job. Once again he knows how to answer the question 'Who are you?'.

Josephine in Nairobi, Kenya

Josephine meets Philippe on a safari in Kenya. He lives and works in New York for an international organisation. Josephine is an IT expert in Brussels. At first, Josephine and Philippe take turns catching a plane to see each other. They do so regularly. They also speak frequently via the Internet. Their relationship becomes serious and they start thinking of children. Choices have to be made. But Josephine is not interested in becoming a stay-at-home mother; her work is too important to her. She is not alone. She meets others in a similar situation. Some have started their own business, others work from home. She talks to her employer. Can she work from home? No, that is not an option. Josephine decides to train as a web developer. When this is completed, she resigns her job. She sets up her own business. In the meantime, Philippe gets a transfer to Nairobi. No problem. Josephine continues to work as a web designer and decides to join him in Nairobi. Shortly thereafter their first child is born. Having household help in Nairobi, Josephine can remain professionally active and be with her family.

For Josephine, the choice is clear. Giving up work is not an option. She identifies strongly with her profession and decides to pursue additional training in order to find a mobile job. She is thus no longer faced with the prospect of having to give up her work and becoming Mrs Philippe.

PART 2

Our stories

Choices made during thirty years at home and abroad

Carine in Kinshasa, RDC

That night, as the wife of a diplomat, I was invited for dinner in Kinshasa. In the background, you could hear the impressive Congo River. The lights on the beautiful Congo-Brazzaville bridge elegantly complemented the evening sun and the exotic birds and crickets confirmed that we were living in a warm country. It was tropical, but a breeze made it bearable. I let the conversation pass me by and admired the beauty of the surroundings. But my ears pricked when I heard my husband say: 'Actually, a person defines himself by what he does, by his profession.' That sentence transported me straight to the core of the theme I had been focusing on for years. He had my full attention. I wrote the sentence down. My husband looked surprised. He was asking himself what he had said that was so special. Over the next few days, I often looked at the sentence and pondered its meaning. We need to split the sentence in two. Yes, a person defines himself by what he does, but that does not necessarily need to be a job. And yes, it is common in our society to identify yourself with your job. Therein lies the challenge: if you manage to change the way you identify yourself, you have already gained so much. There are so many things you can 'do'.

Of course, you would prefer all the aspects from Part 1 to be fulfilled when you go abroad. But can you keep them? Looking for work in a totally new environment often requires the loss of one or more aspects. By setting priorities and letting go of things, you increase your chances of finding work experience whilst abroad and thus get a lot more satisfaction from your stay. What were the choices of Carine and Marie? What was important for them over the years and what motivated them? Perhaps their stories can be a source of inspiration.

Carine's story

Ghent – before the first departure

With a master's degree in history and a teacher training qualification in higher secondary education, it was not easy to find work in the early 1980s. I preferred to be in the classroom, but at the time there were no vacancies for someone in my area of expertise. After a few difficult years on the job market with periods of temporary work, unemployment and further studies for an advanced master's degree in company auditing (evening classes at the Free University of Brussels), I finally found work as a notarial assistant. I loved the job. And then came the phone call, confirmed by a letter a few days later: my boyfriend Bart, now my husband, had passed the diplomatic exam. I was happy for him, of course. A whole year of exams had preceded it. But what about me? It would be hard for me to give up work.

1988 – the first departure: to Kuwait – 26 years old

We were young and inexperienced and had no idea what diplomatic life entailed. Adventure awaited and I did not dwell on the question of whether I would ever work again. Salary did not seem to be the priority at the time. We had never earned much money. We were not used to luxury and lived in a dilapidated house in the city. The professional movers were visibly surprised when they came to collect our meagre collection of household goods. I had not thought about the development of professional skills. What was most important was financial security. We came to a decision: first off, we got married. We also signed a marriage agreement in order to have legally binding arrangements in place in the event of divorce or decease. It may not sound very romantic, but it is essential. We bought an apartment and took out life insurance. That gave me financial support, which brought calmness and certainty. Now I could leave with peace of mind. As for the rest? There was only the adventure. I put all other aspects of my career in my refrigerator far, far away.

What was my priority? Financial security.
What did I put in the refrigerator and what did I actively keep on my plate?

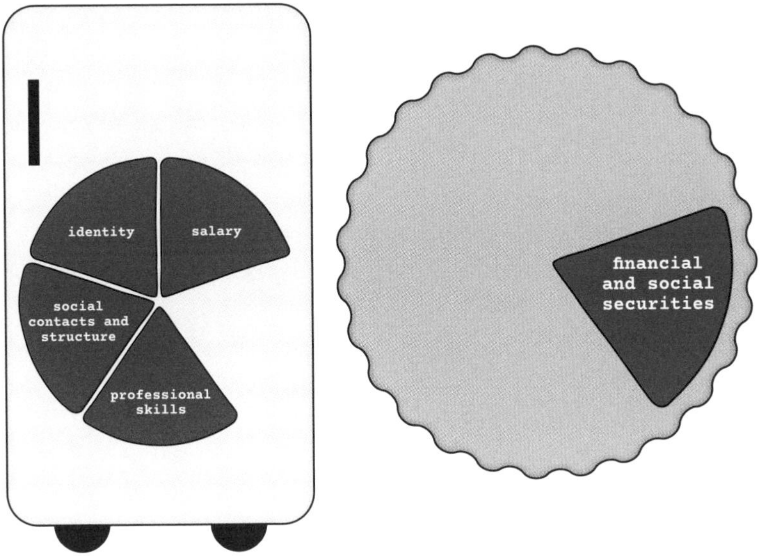

Intermezzo – back in Belgium in 1990 and departure to Vienna in 1991

I was back in Ghent sooner than expected. Saddam Hussein had written a chapter in the history of the world, and one in the history of our family. He invaded Kuwait on 2 August 1990 and that changed the course of our lives. In the meantime, I was a young mother and expecting a second child. After three weeks, I managed to flee with our ten-month-old baby in a convoy of five cars via Iraq to the Turkish border. Bart remained in Kuwait to man the embassy. The refugees on the border between Iraq and Turkey are still etched in my mind, as is the scorching heat and the tension when we were not allowed to cross the border. Back to Mosul for an overnight stay. The next morning, we reported that we would once again try to cross the border. Mobile phones did not yet exist. Communication with the Belgian embassy in Baghdad was difficult and intermittent. Only the women and children, including my baby and myself, along with two drivers, Khalil, a Palestinian, and Molly, an Indian, would try again. The other men returned to Baghdad. When we set out in Kuwait, I had swiftly promoted the Indian driver assigned to me to the status of 'nanny'. Once I was behind the wheel, I was back in control. The inexperienced Indian was a health hazard and I wanted to reach Turkey safely. Slowly, we drove through no man's land. What a relief when we could cross the border and were welcomed by a team of Foreign Affairs officials from Brussels. Months of worry, waiting and uncertainty followed, until Bart's safe return in December, just before the birth of our second son. In the summer of 1991, after six months back in Belgium, we left for our next destination: Vienna.

1991-1995 – Vienna

What a difference from Kuwait! Gone were exoticism and adventure. Order and regularity prevail. Appointments need to be made at least a week in advance, even if all you want is to enjoy a simple coffee with your neighbour. The metro is always on time, and even when it is only a minute late, the Viennese check their watch with a stern gaze. The climate is wonderful. And there's so much culture.

During the first year in Vienna, I felt a growing need to do something outside the house. I felt too locked up as a housewife with two small children. One went to sleep when the other woke up and vice versa, and I found domestic life too claustrophobic. I needed human contact and the ability to socialise without the presence of my children. I took German lessons, but that was not enough. Fortunately, during the second year, I had the opportunity to teach Dutch as a foreign language to Belgian French-speaking children at the French school. It was quite a challenge, since I did not have a language diploma. I developed new skills: teaching a language is not at all the same as teaching history. It was only a few hours a week, so the pay was modest, and I was on the road for a long time, but that did not bother me. I loved the two-kilometre walk through our beautiful suburb to the metro station, and I enjoyed every moment on the train to the city. I opted for the development of new professional skills and for contact with students and parents. We had resolved the issue of 'financial security' before our departure. At that time, the 'identity' aspect was not yet important. That was to come.

What was my priority? Social contacts through work and the development of professional skills.
What did I put in the refrigerator and what did I keep on my plate?

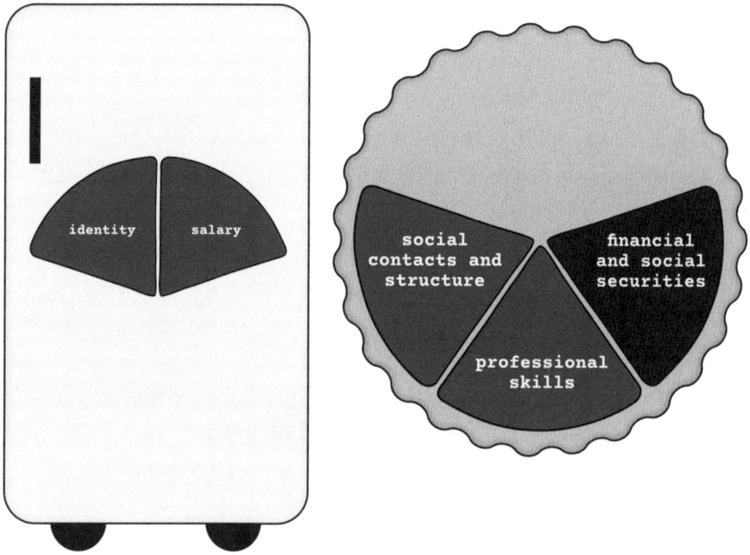

1995 – back to Belgium

After four wonderful years in Vienna, we returned to Belgian reality. We bought a house in Ghent, our home base. Salary was suddenly central. Abroad, my husband's salary was enough for the entire family. Back in Belgium, it no longer was. My previous employer took me back as a full-time clerk. But at the time, there was still little talk of flexible working hours, and other things had changed in the meantime. The situation on the home front was also no longer the same. Because of the changed family situation of children who needed time to get used to the new environment, a child with behavioural difficulties, and a spouse who worked long hours and often travelled, with a heavy heart, I decided to resign.

Thanks to the skills I had learnt in Vienna – teaching Dutch as a foreign language – I was fortunate enough to find a part-time position in adult education reasonably quickly. It also proved easier to combine this with family life. I maintained my financial security. My professional skills grew, because I was teaching adults now. It dawned on me that I did not want to be a housewife. Back in Belgium, I no longer lived in an expat world where, in those days, it was almost self-evident that you didn't work. I realised that I had been given a professional opportunity in Vienna and that I could not let those skills go to waste. Teaching has always been my passion and by teaching Dutch as a foreign language I developed a profession that I could easily take to our next destination: a mobile career! Not working was suddenly no longer an option. The fact that I also had a lot of social contacts was a nice bonus. The puzzle was again completed.

Where was my priority? Salary and developing professional skills. And I kept everything on the plate. My refrigerator was empty!

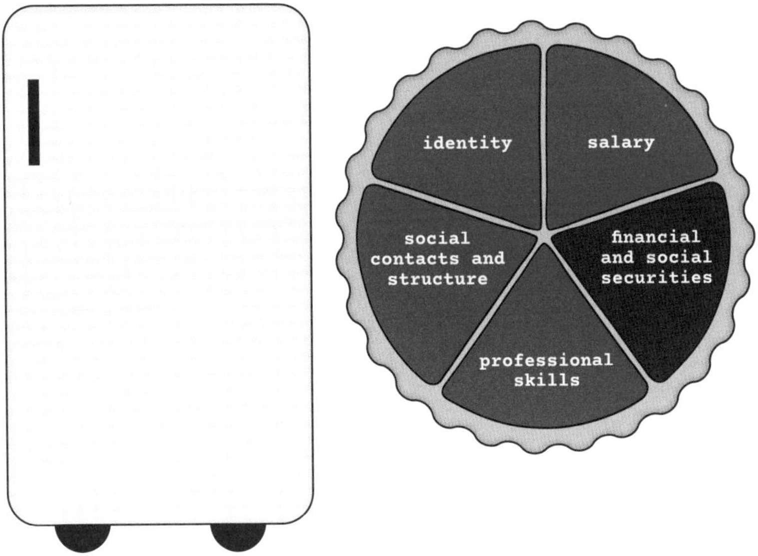

2000 – Paris

Paris! Now that was a treat. We found a beautiful house under the oak trees in Le Vésinet, a Parisian suburb. In the village, which was easy to reach by bike, you could get everything: delicious bread at the bakery, charcuterie, freshly made chocolate ... During the first few months, the summer cycling tours along the Seine really gave us a holiday feeling. On top of that, the heart of Paris, where we could fully enjoy the cultural life, was only twenty minutes away by RER. Through the embassy, we were often invited to theatre performances, vernissages and concerts – often in the best seats. Living like a king in France: there really is such a thing.

For me, a lot changed. My husband and the children were away all day. The children's school was not nearby. They left early with the school bus and often had late Dutch lessons. I had a lot of time on my hands and soon I was looking for an activity outside the house. I did a lot of voluntary work. I was an auxiliary librarian in the history department of the library of the children's international school, and as an active parent I carried out other tasks at school. In our municipality I was assisting the welcoming of English speakers (this way I was able to improve my French and English skills), and lastly, I taught Dutch as a foreign language to a fellow expat. After two years I finally found a paid assignment teaching Dutch as a foreign language. It didn't matter that it was only a few hours a week. But the salary did matter. Not because I needed the money, but because I had the growing feeling that paid work was recognised socially, and voluntary work was not.

What was my priority? Social contacts and the development of professional skills.
What remained on my plate? And what went into the refrigerator?

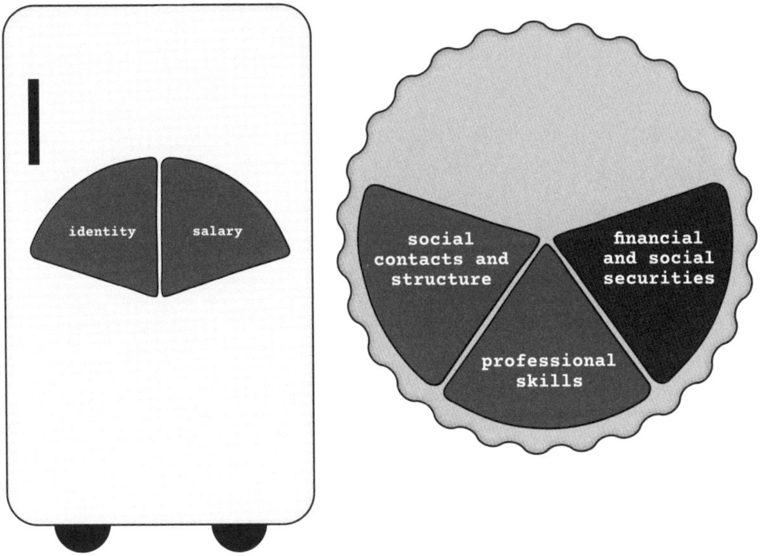

2004 – departure to Geneva

The choice of Geneva was mainly made by our sons. During the family meeting to discuss our next destination there were loud protests against Bart becoming an ambassador in Eastern Europe. The kids wanted to return to Belgium. The only acceptable alternative to our long-haired, recalcitrant adolescents was, in the end, Geneva ... so Geneva it was.

When we arrived in Geneva I thought we would return to Belgium afterwards. In Belgian diplomacy, you return to the central administration after two consecutive overseas postings. As I grew older, I became aware that paid work was increasingly important to me. Not because of the salary, but for my identity. After all those years of voluntary work, it was clear to me that I wanted paid work on our return to Belgium. Why? First and foremost, for my self-image: could I still secure a full-time contract? Secondly, I wanted to be regarded as complete. This has everything to do with the external factors that influence your identity, as we explained in Part 1: the way others see you, the influence of society on you and how you interact with your community. As an individual, you are not isolated from society. Your social and cultural context co-defines who you are and how you evolve. Through paid work I not only wanted to prove to myself what I was capable of, but I also wanted to 'belong'.

Action was needed! The prospect was a return to Brussels in 2008. I would be 46 years old. My last chance to return to the job market, I thought. And what with that patchwork of a CV of mine, it seemed like mission impossible unless I could polish it up. I deliberately looked for voluntary work that would sharpen and improve my professional skills. I became the coordinator of secondary education at the NTC (Dutch language and culture) so that I could enhance my organisational and pedagogical skills. Occasionally, I was a substitute teacher. I wrote the reports of the Parent-Teacher Association meetings at school. The reports were in English, so it was an excellent language exercise. I worked on the IT backlog as database manager of the fundraiser team of the United Nations Women's Guild in Geneva. And during the final year, I found a paid teaching assignment as a Dutch teacher for four hours a week.

These were all good additions to my CV. It was more than a full-time job. Armed with this I was confident of getting back into the job market. The fact that I had a lot of social contacts through all those activities was a nice extra.

What was my first priority in Geneva? Developing professional skills. What did I keep on my plate? And what went into the refrigerator?

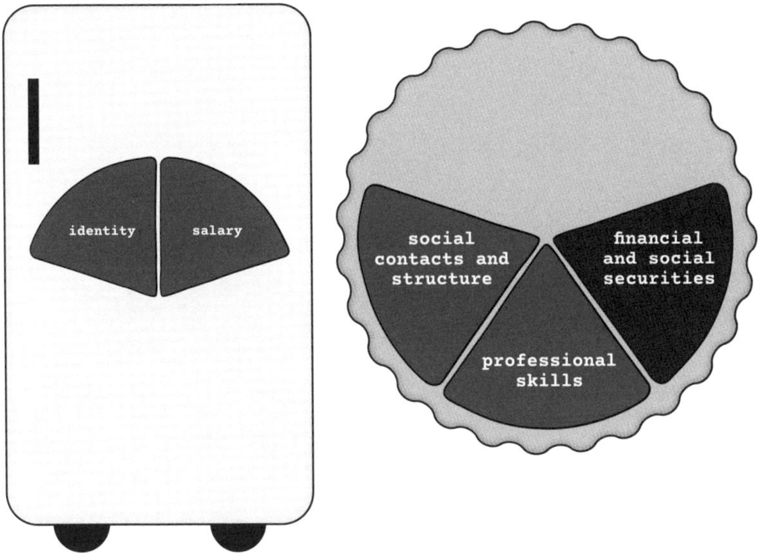

2008 – return to Brussels – 46 years old

Paid work was an absolute priority, so I started to apply for jobs from Geneva. I had my contract before setting foot on Belgian soil again. As a family officer at the Personnel Department of Foreign Affairs, I was able to convert my experience overseas into supporting the families of Belgian diplomats before, during and after their time abroad. Because of the experience I had gained in the field, both through voluntary and paid work, I was confident enough to apply. Instead of a mobile career, a patchwork career gradually emerged. Teaching faded into the background and a completely different job took its place.

Identity was central. I wanted paid work because it brings social recognition. It also went hand-in-hand with what you would expect of an independent woman in the twenty-first century. It was necessary for my self-image. These two facets are key components of your identity. Developing professional skills was also paramount. The fixed structure of an office job and the many contacts made the picture complete.

What was my priority? Identity! The refrigerator was empty again!

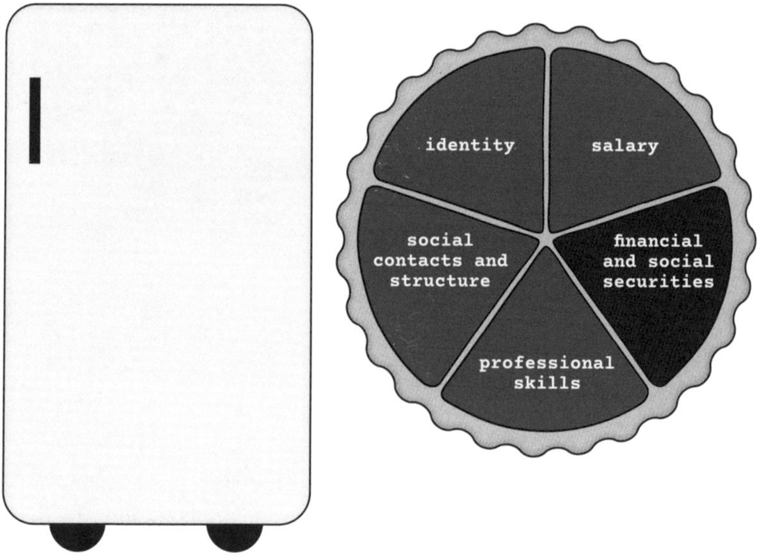

2011 – departing for Nairobi

After so many years in Europe, I was eager to sign up for something more exotic. When my husband was appointed ambassador to Kenya, that wish came true. And it really became a dream destination. We thoroughly enjoyed discovering one of the most cosmopolitan of African capitals. Traditional British-style clubs, a diverse Kenyan and international circle of friends, safaris in Africa's pristine game parks, the beautiful climate, the rich African culture and, on top of all that, an elegant French-style house in a small park full of tropical plants.

But what was I going to do there? Gardening was not exactly my cup of tea. Teaching Dutch again? Would there be any takers? Questions were piling up. After three years as a family officer in the human resources department, a paid job was no longer a priority. I once again knew what I could (and could not) do. Now I wanted to make other choices. Thanks to my experience as a family officer, I was able to think clearly about the five aspects of work and the other benefits of being overseas, and I wanted to use that knowledge more consciously. In the meantime, I started learning Swahili and took golf lessons.

Nairobi was our first time in Africa, and I wanted to get to know the local people. I could have taught European children or adults again, but this time I was looking for a project with Africans in an authentic Kenyan environment. Now that the children had left home, I also wanted the freedom to travel regularly in the region. I often accompanied Bart on his business trips and made myself useful as delegation photographer, a new hobby. It was excellent for the embassy's communication, but also a terrific opportunity for me to explore the most inaccessible places in Africa and portray the traditional culture and beautiful people.

The solution I found was as a voluntary assistant history teacher and librarian at New Dawn high school in a slum in Nairobi. I obtained all the flexibility I needed, and yet it was quite a challenge. Voluntary work was my only option, because I could not get a paid job in a local school (the Kenyan government did not allow it) and my Belgian employer did not allow me to do paid work during my career break. But what an enriching experience it was! As a European teacher, I had to weigh up every word carefully. Everything I know about history was called into question. I had to discard the Eurocentric view. How can you talk about the 'discovery of Africa' to a people that has been living there for centuries? Or 'the New World'? Things became pretty intense during lessons about the slave trade or colonisation, and I loved answering the challenging questions from students whose parents had lived through the colonial period. I remember the gaze of one pupil who wondered in astonishment how the Europeans could have treated Africans the way they did. 'Why?', he asked. As a white person you can feel the weight of history at such moments.

Soon two other projects in other neighbourhoods followed, because the social needs of young people in a city like Nairobi are enormous. I helped set up a library in a social project in the middle of Sinai, a large slum in the industrial district, which had the dubious reputation of being one of Nairobi's most dangerous places. Just getting there was a major undertaking. You could take the car to the police station on the edge of the slum, but my driver and car had to remain there. The car needed to be guarded otherwise I could be faced with an unpleasant surprise on my return. Mirrors, car tyres, even the entire vehicle could be stolen, stripped down and on display the next day on a shop shelf as spare parts. The project staff guided me through a labyrinth of alleys where you had to be extremely careful where to put your feet. At the centre of the district several artists had rented a small building made of corrugated iron – yes, you also have to pay rent for those shacks – where they organised all sorts of creative activities for the children of the neighbourhood during the weekend and after school. A library gave the children the chance to read and a quiet place to do their homework. The latter in particular is often a problem for children in slums, where electricity and silence are a luxury.

Kenyan teachers often asked me to help at their school; for example, one of New Dawn's history teachers lost his job. As an unemployed teacher one way to get a job is simply to start your own school – there is always a shortage of cheap schools. You charge 'school fees' and keep it running with very few resources. (It is, however, more lucrative if you start your own church as an eloquent priest.) My previous experience with libraries made it easier.

I did it all on a voluntary basis. I had decided that this was important for my identity. I always answered the question 'what do you do?' with the story about my voluntary work in those slums. The gratitude I received from the local people was worth its weight in gold. I had a strong need to contribute to society, for my self-image. After a few months I had carte blanche in an area where my car and I had initially needed to be protected: 'Everyone in the neighbourhood knows you, Carine, and everyone knows what you do for us and that you respect us. You can always come here, and you won't be hurt.' I could not think of stronger credentials!

What was my priority? Social contacts, professional skills and identity. What remained on my plate and what in the refrigerator?

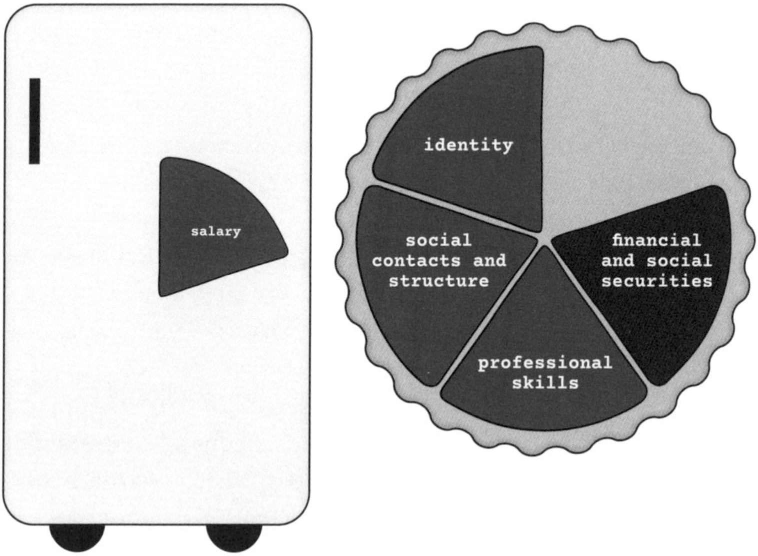

2014 – back to Belgium

During our stay my father-in-law died, and my husband wanted to return to Belgium after Kenya because of his elderly mother. I had taken a career break and was able to return to my job at Foreign Affairs. Moreover, I thought I could grow a lot in that job. I preferred to grab this opportunity rather than be unemployed again in Belgium after an extended period abroad. I was not yet ready for that. And so, after three years in Nairobi, we returned to Ghent and I seamlessly connected with my previous colleagues and the job in Brussels. I went for it with renewed energy and managed to steer through some reforms that I had not been able to achieve when I was a newcomer in federal government service.

What was my priority? Identity and professional skills.
What remained on the plate and what went into the refrigerator?

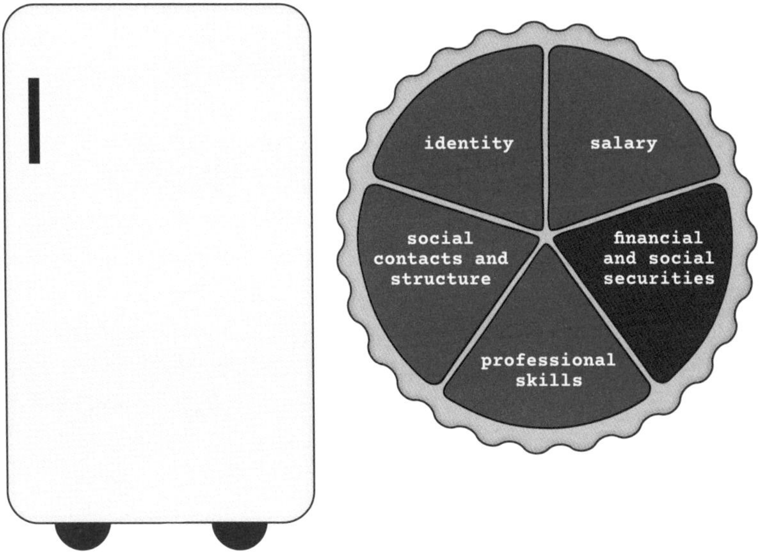

2016-2018 – Kinshasa

Sometimes my plans help determine my husband's destination – or is that a little exaggerated? The idea of writing a book, which originated in my office in Brussels, certainly helped determine the choice of Kinshasa: there I would find the time to develop the project. Whether it was feasible, or whether I would get the book published, let alone make money from it, was unimportant. Writing a book was something completely new, and the teacher in me felt the need to transfer knowledge and skills to interested people and future generations. I had developed this model and would regret not sharing it with others. Even if only one person gains insight or inspiration from the model, it will have been well worth the effort.

Once in Congo I got started. But writing is something you do alone, at your desk. The task isolated me socially and that had never happened to me before. I had to find a solution. Fortunately, there are many associations in Kinshasa where I quickly met pleasant people, and found friends to play golf with and form a class to learn Lingala. It's nice to know that you can also organise your life in a fun way.

The need to actively do something with local people was still very much present. At first, I did not dare commit for fear of lack of time: the book took priority. But I could not resist the urge, and after a year I became a volunteer in a project for street children where I helped with literacy lessons. Yet another new aspect to teaching: another issue with a special target group. It was quite challenging, but the educators' enthusiasm was encouraging and the gratitude of the children who live on the streets and are so happy with the attention you pay them gave me great satisfaction. Their thirst for knowledge was unquenchable.

What was my priority? Professional skills and identity.
What remained on my plate and what went into the refrigerator?

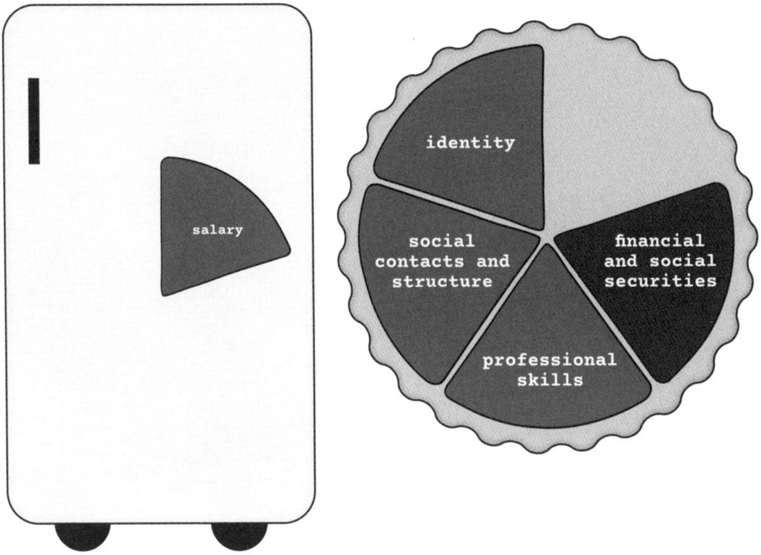

2019 – in Ghent for a while, pending the next destination

During the transition period between Kinshasa and Bamako, this book was a blessing. It was an uncertain and emotional period. I left Kinshasa in a rush in December 2018 to help a dear friend during the final days of her life, not knowing if I could return to Kinshasa because of the political situation there and what was to come. After a few weeks, my husband also left Kinshasa in a rush. He was recalled by the head office because the DRC government wanted to expel him. Fortunately, I had prepared the relocation and in 48 hours, everything was packed and loaded into a container, and Bart arrived at Brussels airport with three suitcases and a golf bag. Would we stay in Brussels? Go back to Kinshasa? Or to another country?

This time, the social aspect was in the fridge altogether. In these turbulent times, I lacked the energy to start new projects. I needed some time out.

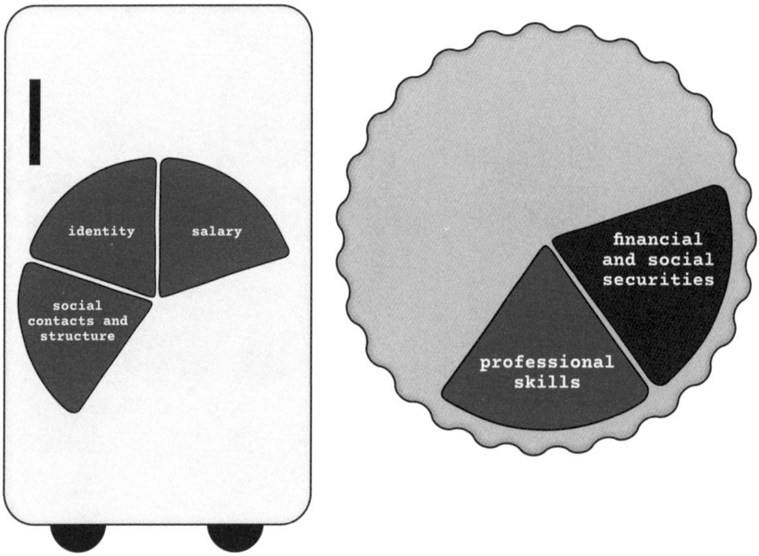

Fortunately, there was this book. Writing became a stabilising factor in those months of uncertainty and bidding farewell. It kept me going. This healing effect is related to my need for flow. I discovered the concept of flow during an expat workshop in Paris and it opened my eyes even more about what work means and could mean. I dare say that this insight changed my life. Is it connected to 'work'? Often, it is, but not necessarily so. Because it is so essential for our well-being and because it is often intertwined with the job we do, we will discuss the relationship between work and flow in the next part.

Marie's story

Before the first departure

Back in 1996, life as a teacher in Don Bosco (a technical school for boys in Brussels) did not make it very difficult for me to say goodbye to my job. I was young and had had a sheltered upbringing; my students were the same age as me, but our worlds could not have been more different. Those few years at Don Bosco left a mark: there, I taught an often unruly group and was pushed out of my comfort zone. I learnt to enthuse, but also to listen, to be patient and to take a lot of things with a pinch of salt. That first temporary job as a Dutch-English teacher made me the mother, diplomat's wife, business manager and journalist that I later became.

It was not only about professional development, but also money. As a very young couple with a baby, every penny was welcome and compared to other jobs a teacher's pay was quite high in those days. The salary gave me the feeling that I was finally able to fully participate in society (identity). There was regularity in my life, and I had pleasant colleagues (social contacts and structure), I learnt a profession (professional skills) and that came with a package of financial and social security. I was a teacher (identity). This work gave me all the aspects that a job entails. Yet I never woke up as happy as the morning after my husband passed his diplomatic exam. I would no longer have to do anything! At the time, I had no idea how strongly my earlier years had shaped me, even less so about what the future would bring. I was enthusiastic and wanted to go on an adventure. I would definitely work again one day, but first I wanted to wait and see.

What did I put on my plate and what did I put in the refrigerator? In fact, I put nothing on my plate and everything in the fridge. But luckily my forward-looking husband took the initiative to review the outstanding balance of the mortgage, so my risk was significantly reduced now that I would no longer have my own income. Bert's employer provided full medical insurance. For a while, we considered transferring the 20% partner premium to a separate account, but eventually we did not see the point. After the recent purchase of our house, saving for a private pension was not possible, at least for the time being.

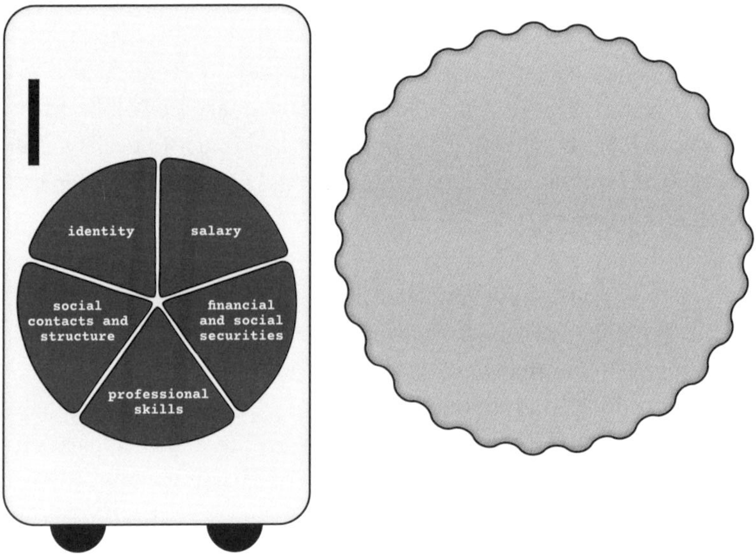

1997-1998 – internship in Budapest, Hungary

In November 1997, I flew to Budapest with an infant and a toddler. My husband was already there. During a longer than anticipated period of nine months, I learnt to move in diplomatic circles. After four years of rough boys and strong language, sophisticated conversation with highly educated people was a relief. But because of that school experience, I kept both feet on the ground, and while I enjoyed my privileged existence, I was also able to put it into perspective.

Yet, as 'wife-and-mother-of', I did not feel entirely complete. I was 27, an academic, and not ready to retire or become some kind of appendix. Our generation of women had learnt to stand on their own two feet. I expected – and also found that others expected it of me – to keep my 'own identity'. During a reception, I met a young Flemish woman who was teaching Dutch at the University of Dubrovnik. We started talking and I told her that I would like to teach again from time to time. She put me in contact with the Dutch faculty at the Protestant University of Budapest. I suggested starting a conversation group. That was a welcome change in my daily life, which had mainly revolved around our two children. I really enjoyed it, even though it was on a voluntary basis. And as is often the case, you fall from one job into another. I cannot recall exactly how things went but, through a connection at the university, I read Dutch words 'with a Flemish accent' on a voice computer for a speech technology company. This was required because the Hungarian company in question wanted to invest in Lernout & Hauspie, a listed Belgian company that has since gone bankrupt. The project did not take long and I think they might have given me a few forints in an envelope, but I found it fun and the salary was not important. I mainly wanted to show that I had a story to tell and could assume a role other than being in the service of my husband and children. I also wanted to have something to do outside the home and away from the diplomatic obligations.

My priority was my identity and other social contacts. I kept these two aspects on my plate.

What did I put in the refrigerator? Salary, professional skills, and financial security.

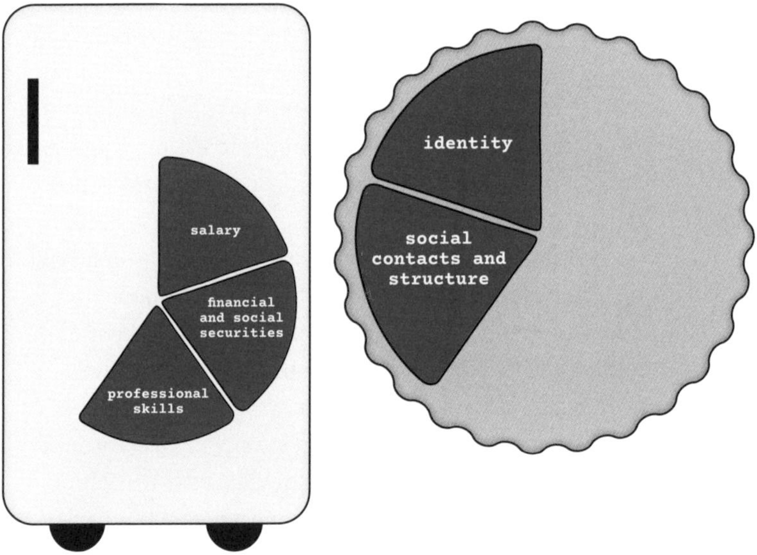

1998-1999 – back in Belgium

In Belgium, it was back to reality. I was pregnant with our third child. I got a job as a teacher less than a week after having registered with the Flemish Employment Agency (VDAB). For a full year I taught Dutch and English again. In the meantime, I gave birth to a daughter. In September 1999 we were sent to Damascus, Syria.

In Belgium, I kept all the slices of pie on my plate.

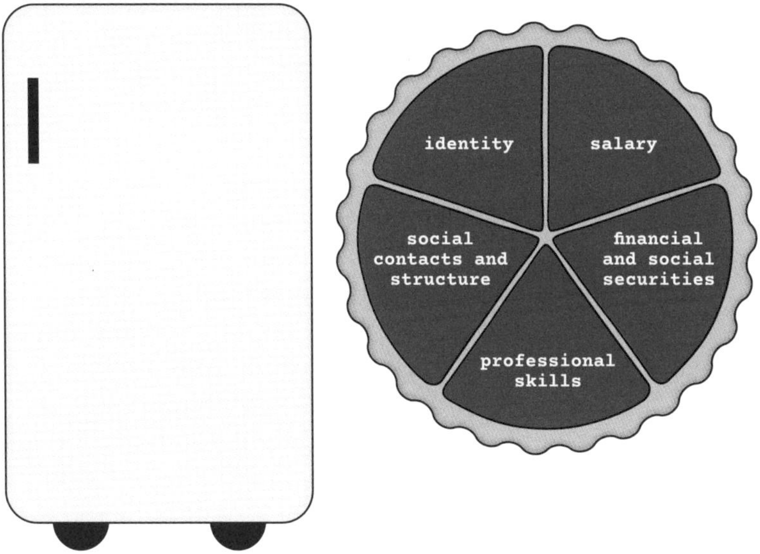

1999-2002 – Damascus, Syria

The first few months in Damascus were pretty intense. Ten days after our arrival, my husband was sent to Riyadh, Saudi Arabia, on a two-month assignment. In the summer, we had been looking for a place to live. We quickly bought a car because the children's school was seven kilometres away. It was logical that we decided to send our children to the French school. But they found French difficult and cried when they had to go to school. It was exhausting. My husband was 1600 kilometres away and I felt alone.

It also dawned on me that I only met people through my husband's job. And because he was not around, and I had just arrived, I hardly knew anyone. Moreover, my French was poor, and I did not like to hang around at the school gate.

That first year, I did not think about looking for a job at all. There were other priorities: making the children happy, reconnecting with my husband. My family was my priority, and I wanted to polish up my French. I registered at two French clubs and every week learnt something new and made new acquaintances. By Christmas, the children had started to speak some French. Our loneliness began to evaporate. And we went out! The rich history, the tasty food, the exceptional hospitality, the complicated social relationships, the do's and don'ts, the fresh strawberries in February: Syria was exotic, and we wanted to get to know the country and its customs. That first year, I put all aspects of a job in the refrigerator.

By the second year the entire family felt at home in Damascus and there was regularity in our life. Now it was time for a job, preferably paid. Minimal financial independence remained a goal for me, more because it was a symbol of my own identity than for the money itself. In our circle of acquaintances, there were several diplomatic wives who worked, including one who had a job at the Office of the High

Commissioner for Refugees (UNHCR). Its focus in Syria was on finding suitable third countries to which to send recognised political refugees (Syria stopped accepting immigrants after the arrival of 500,000 Palestinian refugees). She told me there was a shortage of people to investigate the background information and verify the stories of the refugees. Once upon a time I had studied Germanic Languages to become a journalist: this seemed to be precisely the sort of work an investigative journalist would do. So I dashed ahead and applied, but it soon turned out to be an illusion: there was no budget for this kind of work and there were no official vacancies. Nevertheless, I pressed on and proposed a win-win: I would do the work for free, master the skills of consulting and verify the sources. I would share my findings with the staff every month so that they could better assess the refugees. Many phone calls later, the head of the organisation agreed.

Every day, I sat in a cold basement at a table with my computer and wi-fi, searching through all kinds of safety reports for the location of roadblocks on the Iraqi roads, for a detailed history of certain minorities, what exactly happened during the handling of the Kuwait crisis, and so on. I found it fascinating. In the meantime, a cordial relationship grew with my salaried co-workers and I was happy to share my knowledge. When a staff member went on maternity leave, I grasped the opportunity: I knew the organisation inside out and was able to ask the right questions. My boss arranged for a UN volunteer statute, which earned me 750 dollars a month. Even though I knew that my predecessor received more than 3000 dollars a month for the same work – her country, Norway, also paid a part of that – I enthusiastically took the job. As a resettlement officer, I had to designate a third destination to recognised political refugees: a country where refugees were still admitted. I developed a calm, open interviewing style and received training on human rights and the Geneva Convention. I wrote reports and remained intellectually challenged. Even now, it remains my dream job. The salary was not important compared to the professional skills and knowledge I gained. With a heavy heart, but with the silent hope that this might be a mobile career, I bid my fantastic colleagues farewell in the summer of 2002.

What was my priority? It was only in my second year that I set my sights on a job. Several aspects played a role, but identity was the most important. I wanted to show that I had something to offer and that I could make a social contribution. I still felt the need to be considered more than just the wife of my husband or the mother of my children.

Additionally, the job offered me the opportunity to develop professional skills that I hoped to be able to use someday. Although the salary was modest, it went a long way in Syria. I was happy with it. My colleagues were fun, and the working hours could be combined perfectly with my family.

What remained on my plate? Even though the first motive was identity and professional skills, this job also brought a salary, social contacts and structure to my plate.

What did I put in the refrigerator? Building financial and social security.

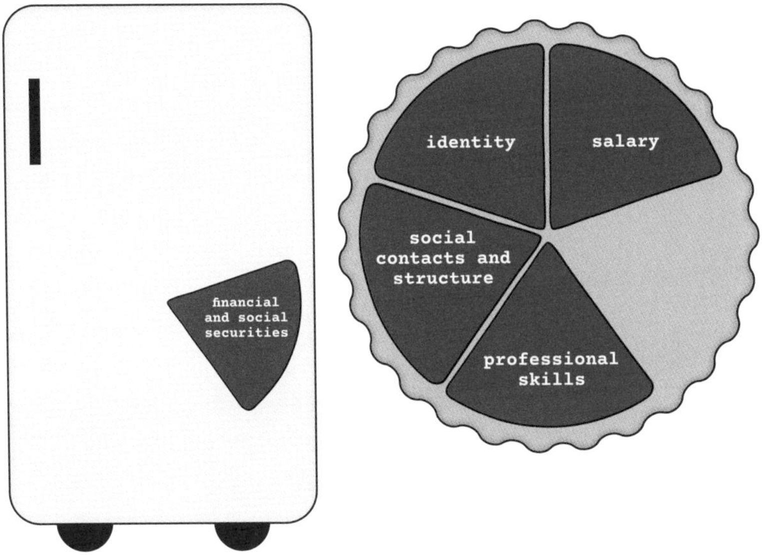

2002-2005 – Ottawa, Canada

In Canada I gave myself six months to get my family life on track before I applied for a job at the UNHCR office in Ottawa. I received no response. Should I write another letter, or would it be better to call? I did not know anyone there, nor could I assess the needs of the organisation. Doubts arose whether a mobile career at UNHCR was actually feasible as an 'outsider' and on the home front there was little enthusiasm for my search for paid work. I let go of the dream of working again for the UNHCR.

At a reception (again) I heard that the Canadian Ministry of Foreign Affairs was looking for a Dutch language teacher to teach staff and spouses who were moving to Belgium and the Netherlands. Teaching two hours a week for three months appealed to me: it fitted in nicely with the needs of my children and I stayed within my comfort zone. Moreover, I received a modest remuneration for it. But I still had a lot of time on my hands.

Slowly but surely it dawned on me that I was procrastinating. I did not read a newspaper because I had to do grocery shopping; I did not do any shopping because I wanted to tidy a cupboard first; I did not tidy the cupboard because a friend came by. It seemed as if I was unable to organise myself between nine and four. The children gave my life a degree of structure ... but I had a hard time with remarks from friends and family that I was lucky to have such a luxurious life. For some time, I had had the feeling that I was no longer involved in conversations. I nodded politely but thought 'what is that person talking about?'. My self-esteem took a battering. At the time, Belgium did not have bilateral agreements with Canada to cover the conditions under which a partner/spouse with diplomatic status could work. I thought that work was not officially possible. Now I know that it is possible if the host country gives its consent, but it is quite a time-consuming process. Maybe studying could give my life some structure and boost my self-confidence? After the necessary English test, I took three courses at Carlton University: introduction to common law, microeconomics, and macroeconomics: unknown territory for me, but common knowledge to many. I passed the exams, had a broader view of the world and, above all, I once again dared to fully participate in discussions at the table.

Later I took on an administrative role at the Dutch embassy (strangely enough, that was possible). Soon I realised that a boring job below my level was no match for my freedom, and I quit after three months. Together with a few other diplomat's wives I spent almost a year organising a show promoting school opportunities for teenage mothers. By prudish North American standards, it was a daring fundraising project. But we brought it to a successful conclusion and raised almost 100,000 euros. While organising the show I learnt: holding meetings, looking for compromises, thinking in terms of solutions, organising logistics, looking for sponsorship. Above all, I surrounded myself with energetic, enjoyable ladies. I did not earn any money, but I enjoyed the experience and learnt a lot of professional skills.

What was my priority? Working in Canada was more difficult. I started looking for opportunities to be 'myself'. Teaching, studying, organising events: they all suited me. The social contacts and professional skills that came with it also proved valuable. During this period, I realised that I would rather not work than have a job below my level.

My pie now looked like this:

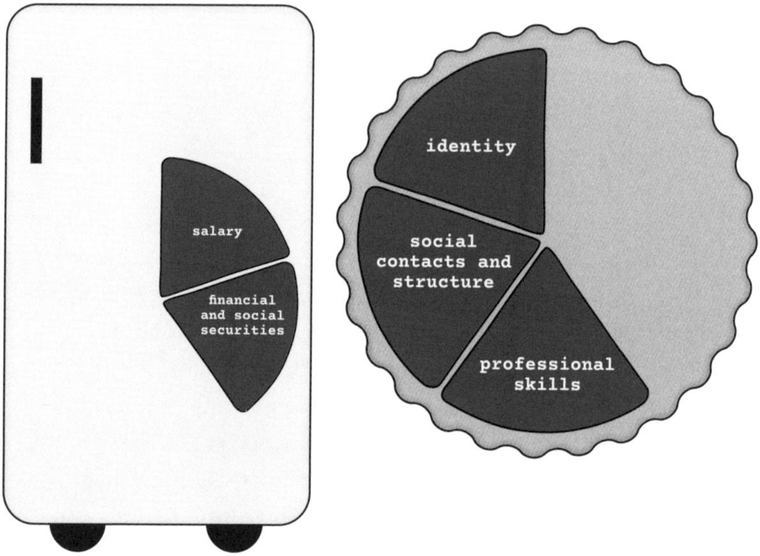

2005-2020 – Brussels, Belgium

With a single civil servant's salary, we were unable to maintain our usual standard of living in Belgium. I was not entitled to unemployment benefits. I sat down at the kitchen table and started applying for jobs. It was quite a funny sight: between 1995 and 2005, I had taught in severall areas in Belgium (Limburg, Brussels and West Flanders), lived in Hungary, Syria and Canada, where I had done at least two jobs each time, in very different sectors. Moreover, I had also started studying again. Recruiters in Belgium had a hard time labelling me: at 35, I was too senior for a junior job; and at the same time I had expertise in nothing and in everything.

The job market in Belgium turned out to be too rigid: either you work in the private sector, for the government or you are self-employed. Fifteen years ago, there was little understanding of a hybrid approach. It was not in the spirit of the times to regard moving a huge amount of goods and chattels as an advanced organisational skill. Nor was your integration into a different culture without losing your own seen as proficiency in flexibility and human knowledge from which, for example, an HR department would benefit. The skills I gained during voluntary work were not considered of equal value. Moreover, the label 'wife of' triggers a lot of prejudice: 'She will want a lot of money, can she handle stress, or criticism?'. I sent spontaneous applications and I focused on the 'Situations Vacant' section in the newspaper. I rarely received an answer.

2006-2012 – six years and five jobs

In Belgium, philanthropy was in its infancy at the time, and there was a need for people who could cast aside their shyness and dare ask for money from the wealthy and generous. In Canada, charity was part of everyday life. I had organised some charity events myself, in Syria and Canada. After three interviews, I found a job as a major donor fundraiser at Greenpeace.

At Greenpeace the challenge was substantial and, despite the success I achieved, I found it difficult. After eighteen months, I co-founded testament.be, through which you can include a charity in your will. Before we launched the campaign, I called hundreds of Flemish people with a questionnaire. It contained very sensitive questions: what was the relationship with their children, had they made a will, did they plan to make one, and would they consider including a good cause in it? I learnt the golden rule of conducting a good interview: keep silent 80% of the time and only talk for the remaining 20%. Gaining the trust of people was a real exercise in using the right words. The atmosphere during the conversation or interview was also important. I think I unconsciously developed my love for extended in-depth interviews here. I learnt a lot of professional skills during this period: interviewing, drafting texts, negotiating, selling ideas.

After missing out on a promotion, I started my own business as a consultant. I could organise my time independently, act as a fundraising consultant to other NGOs, and I wanted to sharpen my professional skills in communication. I contacted the communication manager of our sponsor, Triodosbank, a sustainable bank that was in full expansion, and started work there. If I wanted to stay with the bank, I would have to give up my independent status. This made me hesitate. Six months later, the head of funding at Bozar (Belgian Centre for Fine Arts) called me and asked if I would like to start a philanthropy programme with them. So off I went again. I launched a few initiatives but without much support from the company. My love for philanthropy evaporated.

It was 2010. When were we going to go abroad again? I wanted to bring my French to a higher level: it turned out to be a real asset in my search for work in Belgium. I set my sights on the Fondation pour les Générations Futures/Foundation for Future Generations, on the assumption that we would stay in Belgium for another year and a half. This small but valuable foundation in Namur promotes sustainable thinking and action. The director was part of my network, I rang him up and said I wanted to do fundraising, provided that I could also develop the communication part in Flanders. I earned a lot less but got the job. I loved my work in Namur: the atmosphere was pleasant, the managers were ethical, the work was particularly relevant to society and I improved my French. Yet I was once again sent in the direction of pure fundraising, and that became more and more of a disappointment to me. When the news came that my husband was going to work for the European Union for a while, I realised that we would remain in Belgium for longer than three years.

I had been entertaining the idea that I would move every three years, so I had not been very career-oriented; nor had I developed a strategy for promotion or more exciting jobs. I was over forty. It was time to pursue my childhood dream.

For eight years, I earned my living through consultancy on major donor fundraising at various Belgian NGOs. Just like teaching or working at a UN institution, fundraising could have been a perfect mobile career, but I chose not to pursue that type of work. My mobile career was yet to come, and in the meantime, my CV had started showing all the characteristics of a patchwork career.

When one starts one's own business, questions about financial and social security arise. It was time to take out pension insurance, among other things. My share of the outstanding balance of the mortgage was 20%, and our house was also a security.

What was my priority? At first, it was the salary. But after eight years abroad, I had no idea what size of salary was appropriate for a particular responsibility. I often felt cheated in my jobs, both in terms of title and salary. But maybe that is what people generally feel. For me, identity is the part that I am most concerned about: a job with social relevance has always been a priority for me – almost unconsciously. That is why I stayed in NGO fundraising for so long. Social relationships at work also became increasingly important: I worked longer in places where colleagues and the employer were pleasant but, over time, the content of the assignment and the professional skills that I wanted to develop were always the deciding factors for change.

In this first period in Belgium, the five aspects were all present. I secured financial and social security by taking out a pension insurance policy. The slices of the pie remained on my plate, but it was as if they were being eaten: some pieces became smaller the longer I worked, such as the importance of social contacts and the salary. Other pieces became larger, such as professional skills: I wanted to learn, to grow, and to fully understand the organisation for which I worked. Identity also retained a strong presence: I wanted to be able to proudly say what job I had, what role I played in the world. Thanks to my independent status, I was able to decide for myself which assignments I took on.

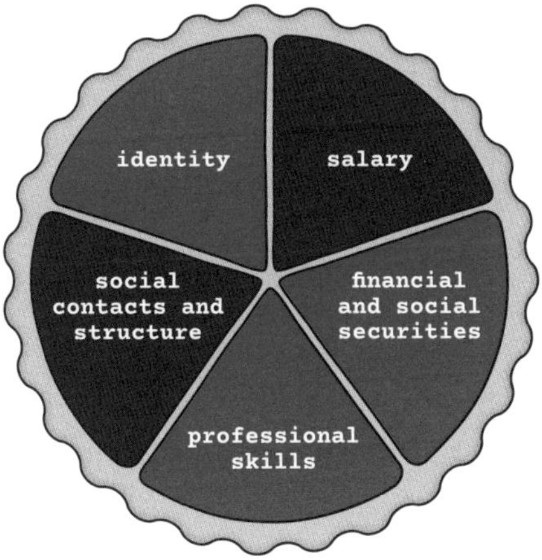

2012-2013 – a new start

In 2012, when it emerged that we would be staying in Belgium for a while, I wanted to stop job-hopping, and instead gain expertise in something enduring. And why not in something for which I once started studying Germanic Languages: sharing stories.

In September 2012, I started a postgraduate master's in journalism. It was a vibrant, yet barking-mad year in which I met people who brought colour to my life. I completely broke out of my regular pattern and put salary and building up securities in the refrigerator. I needed this period to gain enough confidence to apply for a job in the media snake pit. It was a total break from everything I had done before. Being back at school full-time, following the discussions of my fellow students, absorbing new information. Every week we had to complete at least one assignment. We dragged cameras around, recorded, edited, showed the results and received feedback. The adrenaline surged through my body for that whole year.

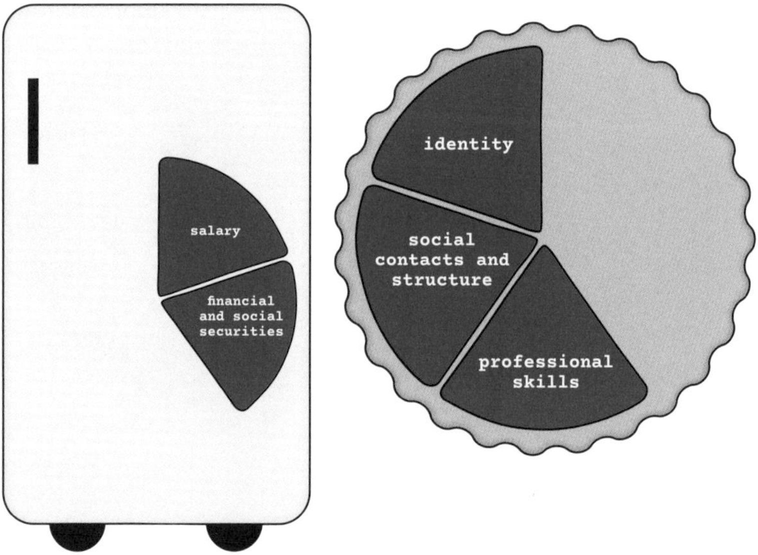

My savings ran out quickly and by June there were only 25 euros left in my bank account. I absolutely needed to find a paid job as soon as possible. Top priority!

2013-2020 – found my mobile career!

Knowing precisely what you want provides direction. Belgian public broadcaster VRT aired an English-language programme aimed at the large expat community in Belgium. That suited me perfectly. Then fortune lent me a hand. During my NGO years, I met a woman who had set up a fair-trade shop; she was now director of the production house that made the expat programme for VRT. Sometimes life is weird. I made sure I prepared well, watched the show online and on TV, and applied ... and yes, I got the position of public relations manager for the programme. Not a journalistic job as such, but one that would evolve over time. With the goodwill of the editorial team, I conducted interviews and came up with new ideas. They were wonderful years;

I learnt a lot about the art of telling stories. But all good things come to an end, and after some severe austerity measures, VRT showed the freelancers the door. Afterwards, I worked on a documentary series for Belgian TV channel Canvas, again thanks to a former colleague. Without my network, I would not have been able to get into a production house by conventional means.

I decided to look for money for my own production. I was, after all, a fundraiser, and I believed it was possible. Somewhere in the Flemish Regional Government there would be a subsidy scheme that matched my project. I prepared a proposal, presented it, and they agreed: I would receive the money, on condition that they could deposit it into a non-profit account. So I founded a non-profit organisation and made the documentary *De kerk in het midden* (The church in the centre) on my own. That project cost me blood, sweat and tears as well as a friendship, but it remains one of the most significant achievements in my life. I now know that I can realise my dreams on my own and I am convinced that I can do so again. This was to be my mobile career.

After making my film, I applied to production houses and came up with ideas, but it proved difficult. So I fell back on my tried and tested approach of calling someone from my network. A woman I had helped out for free with her social project a few years earlier wrote for the monthly magazine *Marie Claire*. I called her and asked if I could translate for the magazine. She was constructive; she told me she had just become editor-in-chief. I congratulated her and asked if she needed anyone in her new team. The position of editor had not yet been filled, maybe I wanted to do that? My mind went into overdrive: *'I'm too old to hesitate, to think that I've never done this before and that I don't know if I can do this. Say "yes", and if I mess it up, they can always fire me.'* I jumped at the chance. It really turned out to be my cup of tea. I can lose myself in it, lose track of time and get a warm feeling. This is what I know how to do and what I want to do. A few years later, she retired and I got her job. I am currently the editor-in-chief of the women's magazine *Marie Claire*.

Work has always been important to me: initially for money, abroad for my identity, and to maintain my intellect and skills. In Belgium, I combined the five aspects, but the significance of professional learning increased. I just kept job-hopping until I finally found what I was looking for in a job: flow.

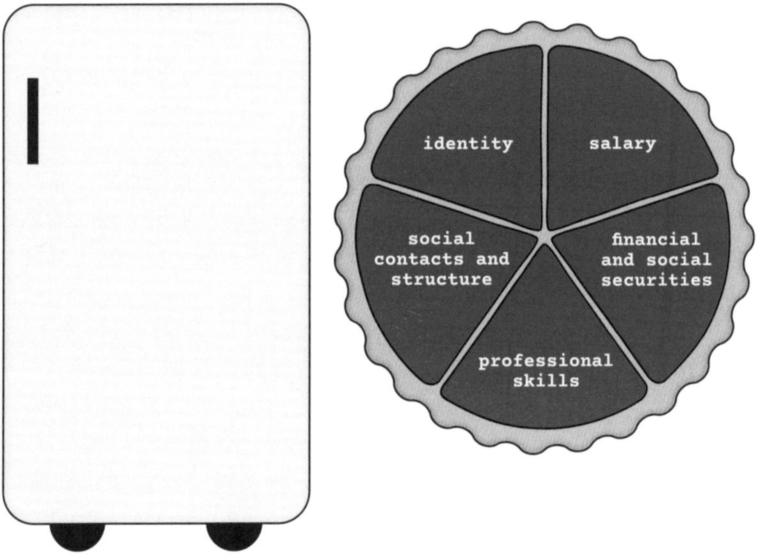

Your story

Take a pen and paper and write your own story. The stories of Carine and Marie are just two examples. Use the pie model and the refrigerator. Your story is bound to be completely different. By writing it down, you will discover why you took on that job at a particular moment, or not; why you missed an opportunity or seized it with both hands; where your priorities lie; and what your options are. Don't hesitate to start all over again. It is not an easy exercise. You will be looking at yourself in the mirror. Take your time.

PART 3

Work and flow

'A joyful life is an individual creation that cannot be copied from a recipe.'

MIHALY CSIKSZENTMIHALYI

What if your work is also your primary source of flow?

Part 1 gives a clear idea of what work means for you today. In part 2, our stories are designed to inspire you to set your own course: how and which aspects of work are or were present for you in different phases of your life? Here they are again:

'Work' gives you:

- a salary;
- social and financial securities;
- development of professional skills;
- a social network and structure in your life;
- an identity.

There is another essential aspect for your personal balance, namely flow. You experience flow while carrying out activities. These can be work-related or take place in your free time.

What is flow?

Flow describes a mental state. You are entirely absorbed by your activities; you are fully involved; you are energised. Furthermore, you perform your task successfully.

The Hungarian-American psychologist Mihaly Csikszentmihalyi specialises in positive psychology, and is the author of this concept. When he carried out research for his book *Flow* (1975), several interviewees spoke of the 'flow that carried them' as a metaphor for blending into their work. So the word 'flow' in positive psychology has nothing to do with the English expression 'going with the flow' (conforming to the majority).

Characteristics

You are in a state of flow when you try to reach a certain goal. Perhaps you achieve this when you paint, play a musical instrument, play sports, or when your studies or work challenge you. The activity is not easy, and you have to use all your skills optimally. By fulfilling the task, you rise above your own abilities and gain new insights. You achieve personal growth.

Csikszentmihalyi identifies eight characteristics when you experience flow.

- » You have a clear goal;
- » You concentrate and are focused;
- » You become completely absorbed in the activity and you forget yourself, you lose your self-awareness;
- » Time flies, you no longer have a sense of time;
- » There is immediate feedback from the activity so that you can quickly adjust your own actions;

- There is a balance between your own skill and the activity to be performed. The activity is challenging but not too difficult to be successfully completed;
- You have a sense of personal control over the situation or activity;
- The activity is intrinsically rewarding.

Many people experience flow at work. Research shows that people spend no less than 54% of their work time in a state of flow. There are, of course, irritating or stressful tasks at work, so you cannot experience flow all the time.

Life consists of a series of good and bad experiences. A good life consists of more good experiences than bad. The best moments are those that bring flow. Csikszentmihalyi describes them as optimal experiences: they are better than the 'good' ones. A cosy evening in front of the TV or a warm summer evening with a drink on a terrace: you may well enjoy it, but it will not bring you to a state of flow. Flow requires your mind and/or body to work hard to achieve a demanding objective. You make it happen. When you are doing so, it can be a real challenge. You might ask yourself: 'What am I doing? Why?' But, thanks to perseverance and concentration on the activity itself, you forget yourself and leave your worries behind. That experience increases the quality of life.

When you experience happiness or satisfaction, you are concentrated on yourself. When you experience flow, you are fully concentrated on the activity. That differentiates flow from feelings like happiness or satisfaction. You will feel satisfied afterwards when the flow experience is over and you have achieved success. Sports, music and many hobbies are full of flow. The marathon runner is pushed to the limit, but while running he forgets himself and concentrates entirely on the objective. The satisfaction is immeasurable when crossing the finish line. The footballer who wants to win the match with his team has a similar experience. His ankle may ache for the rest of the day after an ugly tackle by an opponent, but he will want to take to the field again. So too the dancer who performs demanding choreography, and, in doing so, pushes his body and mind to the limit. The list is endless: bird-watcher, gardener, miniature aircraft builder, actor, musician, painter, mountain biker, chess player, gamer: the list goes on. Look at your friends and acquaintances and the list will quickly grow. These activities all result in optimal experience. They are the currants in the usually boring porridge that is life, as Csikzentmihalyi mentions in his book.

When do you experience flow?

You obtain 'optimal experience' or flow inside and outside work. A paid job involves spending at least a third of the day at work. If you have had 'optimal experiences' at work before going abroad it is self-evident that you will be left with a vacuum when they disappear. How are you going to fill all the free time you suddenly have? The challenge has doubled.

Expat partners are not alone in having to deal with this. You face the same difficulties when you lose your job, have a long-term illness, or retire.

Perhaps free time will bring optimal experiences? According to Csikszentmihalyi's research, that will be a challenge. Ironically, work brings more satisfaction than leisure time. That is because – as is the case with flow activities – work involves intrinsic goals, generates feedback, comprises rules and challenges that match our skills, and gives you a sense of control. This encourages you to become involved to the extent that you concentrate fully and lose yourself in the job. Spare time, on the other hand, is not structured, and it requires more effort to achieve those conditions. That said, hobbies that require skill, and involve clear goals and discipline help to transform the recreation into flow.

This is the key challenge for anyone who is suddenly out of work and who, up to that point, achieved a lot of flow from the job, had little spare time, and experienced little or no flow during leisure time. The current generation of expat partners often belongs to this category. You are highly educated, very active professionally, and then suddenly stuck 'at home'. What are you going to do? By going abroad, you are faced with the task of restructuring your life. You ask yourself questions about whether to work or not. You need to find flow without the fixed structure that your previous life enjoyed.

Flexible-flow and central-flow people

Not everyone experiences flow at work. Yet they too can be happy. We support the stoic idea that if you cannot change the situation, you can still determine your attitude towards it. Or as Carine always says: 'If you can't change it, change the way you think about it.' You can control what you think, feel, desire and do. And while you can try to influence what another person thinks, feels, wants and does, you cannot 'do' anything about it. The other person has to do that himself. If you have your own thinking under control, you can change it. You can look at a situation differently. If you go abroad and you have to give up your job, you could regard it as a serious limitation to the development of your career, but you could also find new possibilities, and explore and embrace them.

This reasoning also applies to flow. How you achieve the optimal experiences in your life is up to you. It could be at work, but it could equally be elsewhere. During the many conversations with expat partners while working as family officer, Carine distinguished two 'types': central-flow and flexible-flow people.

» Either: flow is inextricably linked to work. Achieving optimal experiences is the centre of your quest for a job. You cannot put flow in the refrigerator. Does that limit your choices? Yes and no. If flow is central, it is best to be more flexible in other areas. This leaves you with many options. You should, however, be more open to retraining, reorientation, underpaid or voluntary work.

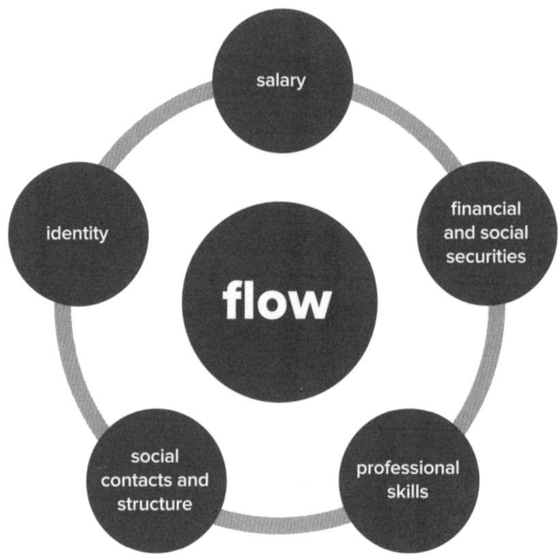

Those who see themselves in this category are central-flow people: flow needs to be there, it is an indispensable condition for doing a job/ activity. Flow is key.

» Or: flow is sometimes part of your work and sometimes it is not, as with the five other aspects. You can achieve flow from your work, but you can also do a job without flow. Either option works for you. This opens up other possibilities. For example, it can help you accept a job that does not appeal to you in terms of content, but for which you are paid, because a salary is important at that moment in your life. Or a job where your professional skills are not challenged. But you continue to work: it is important for your CV and for when you return to your home country. In that case, you achieve your flow from other activities outside work, during your spare time. You are a flexible-flow person.

The currants in the porridge

You decide what your professional life looks like during your time abroad. Depending on the circumstances, you make choices that are tailor-made for you. If you add flow to your search for work abroad, you add an ingredient, namely currants, to your pie recipe. (Every person has a unique formula.) In our model, the pie pieces represent the different aspects of work. The currants symbolise your flow.

What works for you? Which recipe is suitable for you at a specific time? How do you use your ingredients?

» If you are a central-flow person, then you will always require flow during your professional activity. Therefore, your currants are in the pastry of your pie. They are always present. They form the basis.

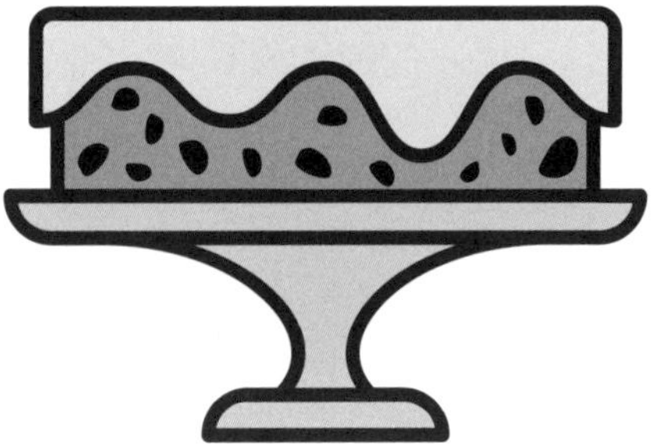

» If you are a flexible-flow person, you sometimes do a job where you do not experience any flow. If you do get into the flow, your currants are in the topping of your pie. If you find a job without flow, the currants will stay in the box and your pie will have no currants. And hopefully you take the box again if you undertake an activity during your leisure time. Because there, too, you can experience flow. In that case, you take your currants with you in your backpack, which is a symbol of your active pastimes.

Both models have equal merit. There is no 'right' choice. Or there is, the right choice is what suits you best at that particular moment.

Stories from the field – looking back at our examples

During their experiences described in Part 2, it is clear to Carine and Marie that they are both central-flow people:

Some of Carine's flow moments:

When I look back at those thirty years of life abroad, I can see that I was unconsciously looking for flow. Without it, I felt apathetic and, above all, bored. I have a great need for flow. When I add the aspect of flow, it is crystal clear how important it has been, and still is, for my personal balance. It is central to me, but it does not detract from the importance of the other aspects.

I see a lot of flow in my own patchwork career as an expat partner: when I was preparing and teaching lessons; when I worked as an assistant librarian; when I searched for the best way to set up – and raise money for – a library in the slums of Nairobi for people with no education; while writing the school plan for the NTC in Geneva and organising lessons; when supervising diplomatic families as a family officer at Foreign Affairs and developing a family policy in the HR department; when searching for a teaching method to improve the literacy of street children in Kinshasa who do not speak French; and also through writing this book. All were optimal experiences involving either paid or unpaid work. Also, while studying languages, whether it was Arabic, German, French, Swahili or Lingala, I had and still have flow. Studying is something I continue to do because I find it an optimal experience.

A few flow moments from Marie

There was always flow in my jobs; I actively sought it. If routine got the upper hand, I came up with a project that challenged me, which assured me of flow. If starting a new project was not an option, I changed jobs. That probably explains the excessive job-hopping. I can lose track of time when doing research work, teaching, preparing and giving presentations, organising and planning group work or events, coming up with solutions, and so on. I look for the fun in my work and can really lose myself in it. I had to set aside the salary, the pension and social security, especially in jobs in the media, in favour of flow. But I also maintained the aspects of identity, development of professional skills and social contacts and structure: these are my three priority aspects.

Hannah, Rob, Krista and Amina

Let's look back at the stories of Hannah, Rob, Krista and Amina from the 'Salary' chapter in Part 1. What does flow mean to them?

Rob in Dakar, Senegal

Rob is a central-flow individual. In Dakar he has a choice to make. He takes on a job that does not challenge him. Administrative work bores him. But thanks to his positive attitude, he is also assigned diplomatic work from which he achieves flow. He finds the tasks challenging but they fascinate him to the extent that he completes the tedious administrative tasks as quickly and efficiently as possible in order to concentrate on political analysis. He completely loses himself in it and forgets the time. He is in control of the situation and his boss is happy with the papers he writes. At that point in his life, he finds it acceptable to have a salaried job albeit one with less flow, because his main goal is to improve his CV. He is still young and wants to find work at the appropriate level at his next destination. During his spare time Rob compensates for the lack of flow: he is an avid chess player. He also looks forward to the weekly football match at the local club. He loves playing with the locals.

Krista in San José, Costa Rica

Krista, on the other hand, is a flexible-flow person. The administrative job at the French school does not particularly challenge her. But the routine work does not bother her. At least she has a job. The salary motivates her and the atmosphere at work is excellent. The fixed structure and contact with colleagues and students are also important to her. Additionally, she has a lot of free time that she sets aside for birdwatching. As soon as she can, she heads into the wild: Costa Rica truly is a birding paradise. She has already created a website with her best photos. Those are her flow moments: her concentration is optimal, she has a clear goal, her sense of time disappears. The enthusiastic reaction of friends and colleagues makes her happy. Maintaining the website is a challenge, but she does it with passion and sees it as an opportunity to develop a new profession. She is thinking of following a postgraduate master's degree in IT. This can be done online. It might even become her mobile career!

Hannah in Nur-Sultan, Kazakhstan

All Hannah wants to do is to design. The salary is not that important. She wants to continue to develop her professional skills. Why? Because when she does, she experiences flow. By continuing to design, she is constantly challenged, and she grows as a person. At those moments, she forgets herself and her family and all her worries. Her flow is optimal and time flies. Every new design brings enormous satisfaction. She is not developing her skills as a means to finding another job as a designer. Maybe this will be the case next time they move. That would be fine, but it does not concern her now. For her, flow is central. As for the rest, she is flexible.

Amina in Berlin, Germany

Amina is also a flexible-flow person. During her years abroad, she opted not to work. She enjoyed time with the children. She felt that she had been too engrossed in her work during their early years. She also used the time to learn languages, to develop her hobby – painting – and to learn to play golf. Painting and golf remain real passions. She can lose herself completely when she stands behind the easel. She forgets everything around her. Back in Berlin, she immediately enrolled at the art academy to improve her technique. And she had golf lessons (improving her handicap remains a constant challenge). Lots of flow moments! But now that the children have left home, she wants to go back to work. She notices that in Germany she does not feel 'complete'. She struggles with who she is. She developed new skills when organising exhibitions abroad. She loves giving guided tours: time flies when she does it. It requires thorough preparation and lots of concentration, but the enthusiasm of her audience is a real encouragement. Now she has flow not only during her free time, but also with her new job.

And what about your flow?

First, ask yourself a few questions:

- Which activities do you enjoy at work? Which characteristics of flow (see point 1) can you link to these activities?
- Which activities at work do you not like? Which flow characteristics are missing from these?
- What leisure activities do you have? Which flow characteristics can you link to them?
- Are you a flexible-flow person or a central-flow person?

Now go back to your story at the end of Part 2. Identify the flow moments in the jobs or activities that you fulfilled, upgrade your pies with a crust or filling, or write your story using your flow like currants in your porridge.

Waking up early to get far can only succeed after a long journey

Malian saying

Closing words

Perhaps you are at the beginning of your journey to 'expat land', or somewhere in the middle. Maybe you are anxious, or maybe you know exactly what the journey will bring. You will not find your way without trial and error, without searching and questioning. As the Malian proverb says, this requires effort. You cannot reap a rich harvest without efforts. We hope this book can help you find the way. It is a search for yourself, for what is or is not in it for you on a professional level during your stay abroad.

This is an activity book. Get started. Be inspired by the many practical examples and our own stories. Analysing our very different situations based on Carine's model gave us a much better understanding of the choices we made, consciously or unconsciously. Write your own story using this simple but effective model. Find out what conclusions you draw and what you want to do with them.

Going overseas is not only a challenge for you as an individual, but also for your relationship. You might split up or grow stronger as a couple. Every expat who takes a partner abroad should also read this book! Without the cooperation of both parties, time spent abroad will not end happily.

Therefore, at the end of this book, we feel the need to give the expat a tip. After all, it is a huge responsibility to drag your partner and your family along on a foreign adventure. To maintain a relationship of equals, it is crucial that you, the expat who goes abroad with the security of a job, continue to respect and value the activities of your partner: also the frequently temporary, underpaid or voluntary work. If you start to regard this as an inferior 'pastime', your partner's well-being and happiness will suffer. Remember that you depart as equals, and your expat partner will expect that to remain the case for the duration of your overseas posting.

Good luck!

Carine and Marie

Acknowledgements

To our husbands, Bart and Bert, who for so long have given us the space and respect to fulfil our own projects.

To Carine and Bart's children, Max and Wolf, who experienced ups and downs during their childhood years abroad but acknowledge the richness of the experience.

To Marie and Bert's children, Cas, Flore and Zita, who owe their linguistic diversity and their tolerant attitude to their childhood abroad.

To the friends we met on our travels, who helped make the stays abroad so rewarding.

To all expat partners who have openly related their experiences during workshops and meetings, and who were the source of inspiration for our stories from the field.

To the family and friends at home who have been following our experiences for all these years and welcome us each time we settle down back home again for a shorter or longer period.

To Linda Hoeben of People On the Move, business coach Hilde Debackere, family officer Hildegarde Van de Voorde, Peter Saverys, Niels Janssens and Lotte Demeyer from LannooCampus, and Graham Muir for their clear advice and constructive feedback.

Useful websites

Some useful links

English

- www.aportableidentity.com: site owned by the authors of the book *A Portable Identity*
- www.expatexchange.com: a platform with a lot of information for and by expats on how to prepare fully for your departure abroad.
- www.expatfocus.com: ExpatFocus is a platform with information and services to prepare your expatriation.
- www.expatwomen.com: network for female expatriates
- www.figt.org: *Families in Global Transition* is a global network specialising in expatriation with an annually rotating conference.
- www.global-connection.info: training and consultancy agency for companies sending out expatriates and their families
- www.globallivingmagazine.com: *The Lifestyle Publication & Resource for Expats Worldwide*: Magazine for expats, published six times a year
- Grumpy Expat: a Facebook group where you can freely, and without being judged, express all the annoyances and difficulties – both small and large – that you encounter when you move to another country.
- www.idcn.info: *International Dual Career Network* supports the dual career of the expat and the expat partner.
- www.iflg.uk.com: *International Family Law Group* provides legal advice on international marriages and divorces.

- **www.internationaltherapistdirectory.com**: network of coaches and therapists specialising in international mobile living, third culture kids and the expat community
- **www.netexpat.com**: training and consultancy agency for companies sending out expatriates and their families
- **www.permitsfoundation.com**: organisation that provides support to expat partners in obtaining work permits
- **www.tandemnomads.com**: a podcast show and platform with tips on how to start your own business
- **www.transitionsabroad.com**: a platform for support in travelling, working, studying and living abroad
- **Two Fat Expats**: a Facebook group where you can ask questions about your expatriation

French

- **www.expat-heroes.com**: The podcast Expat Heroes gives expats the opportunity to describe how they adapted abroad and what they achieved.
- **www.expat.org**: a platform with information, current affairs and tips regarding expatriation
- **www.femmexpat.com**: a network for French speakers abroad, including Facebook groups
- **www.fiafe.org**: a network of local associations specialised in the arrival of French speakers abroad
- **www.lepetitjournal.com**: a digital newspaper with a focus on international life
- **www.ufbe.be**: *Union Francophone des Belges à l'étranger* is an association of French-speaking Belgians abroad.
- **www.ufe.org**: *Union des Français de l'Etranger* is an association for French citizens abroad.
- **www.expatvalue.com**: Through a platform and a Facebook group, ExpatValue supports expat partners in their professional career abroad.

Multilingual

- www.expatclic.com: a platform for and by expat women in English, French and Spanish
- www.easyexpat.com: a platform for international mobility in nine languages, including Dutch

For children: TCK – Third Culture Kids

- Expat Parents: a Facebook group where parents can share tips on children and expatriation
- www.interactionintl.org: site of David Pollock, co-author of *Third Culture Kids*; specialisation: TCKs and their families
- www.tckworld.com: site of Dr Ruth Hill Useem, specialised in third culture kids
- www.multilingualparenting.com: website of Rita Rosenback, author of the book *Bringing up a Bilingual Child*

Bibliography

Bailleul, Père Charles. *Sagesse Bambara. Proverbes et sentences.* Editions Donniya , 2005.

Brayer Hess, Melissa & Linderman, Patricia. *The Expert Expat. Your Guide to Successful Relocation Abroad.* Nicholas Brealey Publishing, 2007.

Bryson, Debra R. & Hoge, Charise M. *A Portable Identity: A Woman's Guide to Maintaining a Sense of Self While Moving Overseas*. Transition Press International, 2005.

Carnot, Alix. *Chéri(e), on s'expatri(e)! Guide de survie à l'usage des couples aventuriers*. Eyrolles, 2016.

Copeland, Dr Anne P. *Many Women Many Voices. A Study of Accompanying Spouses Around the World.* The Interchange Institute commissioned by Prudential Financial, 2004.

Csikszentmihalyi, Mihaly. *Flow. The Psychology of Optimal Experience*. Harper Perennial, 2008.

Csikszentmihalyi, Mihaly. *Finding Flow. The Psychology of Engagement with Everyday Life.* BasicBooks, a division of HarperCollins Publishers, Inc., 1999.

Expat Communication. *Le livre blanc*, 2015. www.expatcommunication.com

Global Connection. *Expat & Partner Guide*. Global Connection, 2011.

Goutain, Gaëlle & Russell, Adélaïde. *Conjoint expatrié. Réussissez votre séjour à l'étranger*. L'Harmattan, 2011.

Goutain, Gaëlle & Russell, Adélaïde. *L'enfant expatrié. Accompagner son enfant à travers les changements liés à l'expatriation*. L'Harmattan, 2009.

McNulty, Yvonne. Being Dumped in to Sink or Swim: An Empirical Study of Organizational Support for the Trailing Spouse. *Human Resource Development International*. 15/4,417-434, 2012.

NetExpat and Ey. *Relocation Partner Survey Report 2018*. Netexpat.com.

O'Shaughnessy, Christopher. *Arrivals, Departures and the Adventures In-Between*. Summertime publishing, 2014.

Parfitt, Jo & Reichrath-Smith, Colleen. *A Career in Your Suitcase. A Practical Guide to Creating Meaningful Work... Anywhere*. Summertime publishing, 2013.

Pascoe, Robin. *A Moveable Marriage: Relocate Your Relationship Without Breaking It*. Expatriate Press, 2003.

Patterson, Jennifer A. *Financial Planning for Global Living. Go Beyond Cross-Border Tax and Legal Complexity to Location Independence, Financial Freedom and True Life Satisfaction*. Make Your Mark Global, 2018.

Pollock, David & Van Reken, Ruth. *Third Culture Kids. Growing Up Among Worlds*. Nicholas Brealey Publishing, 2009.

Reber, Deborah. *In Their Shoes. Extraordinary Women Describe Their Amazing Careers*. Simon & Schuster, New York, 2015.

Rosenback, Rita. *Bringing Up a Bilingual Child: How to Navigate the Seven Cs of Multilingual Parenting*. Filament Publishing, 2014.

Storti, Craig. *The Art of Crossing Cultures*. Boston. Nicholas Brealey Publishing, 2001.

Storti, Craig. *The Art of Coming Home*. Boston. Nicholas Brealey Publishing, 2003.

Talleux, Stéphanie. *Conjoint d'expatrié votre carrière continue!* Groupe Studyrama. 2012.

Tissot, Juliette. *Indian Therapy*. Novel. Editions Tensing, 2015.

Tollenaere, Natalie. *L'Art des Possibles. Créer son chemin dans une vie internationale mobile*. Summertime Publishing, 2010.

Tollenaere, Natalie. *The Art of Possibilities. Creating Our Path in an International Mobile Life*. Summertime Publishing, 2010.

Wiles, Louise & Simpson, Evelyn. *Thriving Abroad. The Definitive Guide to Professional and Personal Relocation Success*. Practical Inspiration Publishing, 2017.